Educating Children with Profound and Multiple Learning Difficulties

Educating Children with Profound and Multiple Learning Difficulties

Edited by
Jean Ware

David Fulton Publishers
London

David Fulton Publishers Ltd
2 Barbon Close, London WC1N 3JX

First published in Great Britain by
David Fulton Publishers 1994

Note: The right of Jean Ware to be identified as the editor of this work has been asserted by her in accordance with the Copyright, Designs and Patents Act 1988.

British Library Cataloguing in Publication Data

A catalogue record for this book is available from the British Library

ISBN 1 – 85346 – 329 – 9

Typeset by Action Typesetting Limited, Gloucester
Printed in Great Britain by the Cromwell Press, Melksham.

Contents

Contributors

Dr Sheila Glenn is Head of Research in the School of Healthcare at Liverpool John Moore's University.

Dr Juliet Goldbart is a senior lecturer in Psychology and Speech Pathology at Manchester Metropolitan University.

Ian Healey was research officer on the ESRC-funded project 'Contingency-sensitive environments and progress of profoundly handicapped children.' He is now a teacher at Downs View School, East Sussex.

Yvonne O'Brien worked with Sheila Glenn on the research described in Chapter 5.

Richard O'Connell is a teacher at Queen Elizabeth II Jubilee School in Westminster.

Dr Jean Ware is a lecturer in Psychology of Education and Special Educational Needs at the University of Wales, Cardiff.

Dr Judith Watson is lecturer in Professional and Curriculum Support Studies, Moray House Institute, University of Edinburgh.

Preface

This book was written for those concerned with the education of pupils with profound and multiple learning difficulties, primarily for teachers, but also for educational psychologists and therapists. Its main aim is to highlight the implications of recent research for classroom teachers, but it also tries to examine the context created for the education of pupils with PMLDs by implementation of the National Curriculum, though that task has not been made any easier by the publication of the Dearing Report barely a month before the typescript was due with the publishers.

The implications of recent developments in four areas are particularly examined: the inclusion of pupils with PMLDs within the general classes of SLD schools; the use of microtechnology; the development of the use of staff-pupil interaction as an aspect of the curriculum, and early communication development. The role of classroom organisation in curriculum delivery is also discussed.

Throughout this book 'pupil' has been used to refer to children and young people of school age. Where there are general references to pupils or teachers the general terms 'they' and 'them' have been used wherever possible; however, most references to teachers and pupils are to specific persons, and they have been referred to as 'he' or 'she' as appropriate. Although there is currently much discussion as to whether it is the most useful way of describing this particular group of people, the term Profound and Multiple Learning Difficulties (PMLDs) has been kept for two reasons: this is a book intended for teachers, and in that context the term 'learning difficulties' adopted in the 1981 Act seems appropriate, and the words 'profound and multiple' stand as a reminder that the pupils with whom this book is concerned have several disabilities in an extreme degree, including a profound intellectual impairment.

I hope the research discussed here will help teachers (and others) provide an environment for pupils with PMLDs which promotes their development and which is enjoyable, challenging and satisfying to work in. Behind all this lies the conviction that people with PMLDs and those who teach them are, above all, persons of infinite worth.

Jean Ware
April 1994

CHAPTER ONE

Conceptualizing Progress in Children with Profound and Multiple Learning Difficulties

Jean Ware and Ian Healey

Introduction

If teachers from an SLD school are asked to talk about the difficulties or frustrations of working with pupils with PMLDs, they will frequently say that one major problem is the apparent lack of progress. Likewise, some parents report that there seems little point in attending school parents' evenings or annual reviews when what they hear is a list of objectives which have not been achieved and will be reset for perhaps the third or fourth term in succession.

My dictionary gives several alternative definitions of 'progress':

> Movement forwards, especially towards a place or objective. Satisfactory development, growth, or advance. Advance towards completion, maturity or perfection...
>
> Hanks (1986)

The idea that progress is about discernible movement towards an objective, as suggested by these dictionary definitions illuminates two areas of difficulty for those who are concerned with children with PMLDs; the definition of objectives and the measurement of movement towards them – ideas central to the whole educational enterprise. It is not surprising, then, that both teachers and parents have difficulty in dealing with the apparent lack of progress made by some pupils with PMLDs. A discussion of progress in relation to pupils with PMLDs therefore seems an appropriate place to start a book of this kind. Such a discussion is important at two levels. At a philosophical or conceptual level it can help us to be confident in what we are trying to achieve with people with PMLDs and at a practical level it can offer methods of assessment which demonstrate progress in situations where more conventional techniques prove inadequate.

Progress and quality of life

The difficulties created by the failure of some people with PMLDs to show measurable progress on conventional assessments is not limited to the field of education; for the idea that progress is essential not just to education but to a worthwhile human life is very deeply rooted in late 20th century Britain. Individuals with PMLDs represent a severe challenge to this belief. Since some, at least, of these individuals self-evidently do not make progress in the generally accepted sense, it seems that either progress cannot be as important as we think, or these people do not have a worthwhile human life. Examination of this wider issue may help us to look at the problem of educational progress from a new perspective.

Historically, it is the view that people with PMLDs do not have a worthwhile human life which has predominated. It is probably fairly well known that in the ancient Greek city states of Athens and Sparta, babies with obvious disabilities were left to die of exposure. This practice may fill us with horror, but, as Tilstone (1991) points out, it is not dissimilar from that current amongst some paediatricians today of providing only 'tender, loving care' to babies with severe and profound learning difficulties.

Research over the last decade has shown that a considerable percentage of paediatricians in a variety of countries regard it as inappropriate to offer life-saving treatment to children who, when so treated, will nonetheless continue to have severe or profound learning difficulties. For example Schultz (1993), comparing responses of paediatricians in Australia, Canada, Hungary and Poland to a questionnaire concerning treatment and non-treatment of 'defective' babies, found that more than 20 per cent of all those responding gave 'brain damage' or 'mental retardation' as examples of conditions which would lead them not to make maximum efforts to preserve the life of an infant. It is however important to realise that the rationale for such decisions has changed somewhat over the intervening centuries. In Sparta, children were seen only in terms of their value to society and those with disabilities (whether intellectual or physical) as lacking value. In Western societies of the late twentieth century, whereas value and cost to society are still considerations in making such judgements, paediatricians give considerable weight to the likely 'quality of life' of the individual. Mitchell (1986) reports that the majority of doctors from the New Zealand hospitals which he surveyed took quality of life into account in making treatment decisions, with some saying it was the most important factor, and Schultz (1993) found that this was the general principle which was 'the significant factor' in paediatricians' decisions to treat or not to treat infants.)

Although there is continuing disagreement about what should be included in this rather vague concept of 'quality of life' (Felce and Perry, 1993), when unpacked it seems to be based, at least in part, on what is generally accepted as 'success,' within Western Society (independence, job, marriage etc). It is the perceived inability of individuals with multiple severe disabilities to achieve or even make any significant progress towards these goals that leads some paediatricians to conclude that their lives are literally not worth living. Tilstone suggests that recent court cases in the United Kingdom support the view that these opinions are shared by the public in general, amongst whom there is still considerable doubt about the possibility of a worthwhile life for people with severe and profound disabilities. Of course the idea that progress means progress towards the goal of a life like that seen as desirable by the majority of society is only one view, but it highlights the fact that inherent in the concept of progress is the notion of a goal towards which progress is being made.

Progress is similarly seen as crucial to the idea of educability. For example, the educational philosopher, White, rejects the notion that progress must necessarily be towards the goal of self-determination pointing out that although this is generally seen as crucial to 'quality of life' in our society, this is not the case in all societies. Nonetheless he re-emphasises the importance of demonstrable learning in his discussion of Warnock's view that the goals of education are the same for all children. (White, 1991).

The first major problem in any discussion of progress is therefore to *agree* about the goals. Quality of life is a social construct, relative to more than one set of criteria. Relative that is, not only to what is seen as desirable by most members of a given society at a particular point in time, but to the needs and desires of the individual. For one individual the need for peace and quiet may lead them to view life in an isolated rural community as being of an enhanced quality; while for another the lack of services in the same community may represent a serious threat to life of a high quality. Furthermore, given changed circumstances, the views of both individuals and societies about what represents quality of life and thus progress towards it may change radically. For example, there is currently a conflict between those who view quality of life in terms of ever-increasing technical sophistication and those who see it in terms of sustainability. Progress towards quality of life for these two groups can sometimes be in opposite directions. There is only a limited degree of consensus about what is meant by quality of life and consequently about what constitutes progress.

Educational progress and curriculum related assessment

This limited consensus about what is meant by 'quality of life' is relevant to the discussion of more specifically educational progress because, while the aims of education are partly about the well-being of society as a whole, they are also partly about enhancing the quality of life of the individual. As White points out, it is difficult to separate these two aspects of well-being since the extent to which an individual is 'flourishing' is usually seen in terms of the extent to which they fulfil socially derived goals. This dichotomy of aims is well expressed in the 1988 Act when it states that the school curriculum should be one which 'a) promotes the spiritual, moral, cultural, mental and physical development of the pupils at the school and of society; and b) prepares such pupils for the opportunities, responsibilities and experiences of adult life.'

Since the curriculum is the means by which the aims of education are to be achieved, it is unsurprising that progress within an educational context is usually seen in relation to the curriculum. But, while most people would agree that education is partly about enhancing quality of life, there is much less agreement about how this is to be achieved in curriculum terms. One (unexpected) benefit of the National Curriculum has been that it has helped teachers of pupils with PMLDs to think about quality of life more widely than simply as the independence or autonomy which characterised the aims of SLD schools in the past.

Wedell suggests that one useful way of thinking about the curriculum is in terms of a 'framework of expectation' (Wedell, 1981). According to this model, the progress of any child can be analyzed by comparing performance with expectation – an idea which has become very familiar in the context of the National Curriculum. In the National Curriculum, as in many other versions of this model, the curriculum is seen as a logically arranged sequence with each element developing out of previously mastered content and leading towards the next and, eventually, to some final goal. A child's progress is seen in terms of the rate at which they master the sequence.

A similar conceptualisation underlies many developmental or basic skills curricula. Whether the sequence is concerned with the development of the ability to eat independently or the critical analysis of the causes of historical events, there is an underlying assumption that the mastering of each element in the sequence is facilitated by previous elements and in turn contributes towards the mastery of subsequent elements. While this may seem like common sense, in practice problems are experienced in reaching agreement on both the sequence of the content and the stage at which particular elements should have been mastered by an individual child. This means that unless the sequence is regarded as provisional and subject to revision in the light of children's progress through it, it may become a straitjacket in which difficulty with one particular element is taken as evidence that the child is not (yet) capable of further learning.

These problems are particularly acute when children with PMLDs are concerned, for they are notoriously poor consumers of curriculum. One of the key aspects of what a teacher of a pupil with PMLDs does, is to make decisions about what elements of the accumulated backlog of curriculum have priority. By doing this, s/he exposes the fallacy of conceptualising curriculum in terms of a linear sequence. It rather resembles a building with the teacher having to decide what materials and features of the structure are absolutely essential, what must be left out and where it is only possible to construct a facade of competence. This process of selection highlights the socially determined nature of the curriculum. Furthermore, educational progress, like progress in general, is relative to more than one set of criteria. What we can call progress seems to be related not only to a body of knowledge, but also to the needs of the person being taught. Consequently, assessing progress by comparison with a general framework of expectation alone is inadequate.

Another, perhaps more major, problem especially relevant to pupils with PMLDs which is highlighted by this notion of the curriculum as a framework of expectation is the assumption that there is some predefined endpoint towards which the sequence leads. The issue then arises as to the position of those who never reach that endpoint. Are the intermediate steps worthwhile achievements in themselves?

Problems with deciding what principles should be used in curriculum sequencing have been discussed for nearly a century, and Posner and Strike (1976) suggest that no satisfactory solution has been found. However, they discuss five *possible* principles on which content can be sequenced, each with a number of subtypes (world related, concept related, inquiry related, learning related, and utilization related). Of these principles, learning related – based on knowledge of the psychology of learning; and utilisation related – based on how or how often content will be used, have been most frequently employed in relation to pupils with severe and profound learning difficulties. However, doubts about the usefulness of achieving (only) intermediate steps in the sequence, especially in relation to independence skills, have led to attempts to reconceptualise the type of sequence involved, and thus the way in which progress is assessed. Most interestingly, Baumgart et al (1982) suggest that the curriculum for pupils with PMLDs can more appropriately be conceptualised as sequences relating to the amount of assistance that the pupil requires to complete the task and the centrality of any sub-components to the overall meaning of the task. They argue that the intermediate steps in sequences of this type can be achievements which in themselves improve the pupil's quality of life. For example, a pupil who is able to indicate a need to go to the toilet is potentially more independent, and able to enjoy a higher quality of life than one who is able to pull up their pants from the knees. However, while this method of arriving at a curriculum sequence may overcome some of the problems involved in striving towards obviously unattainable goals through intermediate steps which have little intrinsic value, it does not address the issue of how extremely slow progress can be assessed. It may prove no easier to demonstrate that our pupil is actually learning to indicate their need to use the toilet than it is to show that they are learning to pull their pants up.

Methods of assessing progress

There are three main issues in the assessment of progress: what we measure to demonstrate that progress has occurred, the instrument we use to measure it and the relevance or usefulness of the assessment in guiding further teaching. This is well illustrated by the prolonged and heated argument about National Curriculum Assessment. Questions have been raised about what is being measured, the nature of the tests and about whether the results of such assessments offer teachers any information which is relevant to further teaching. Of course these three aspects are not entirely independent, but it may nonetheless be helpful to consider the adequacy with which any particular method of assessing progress deals with each of them.

The forms of assessment currently most widely used with people with PMLDs are checklists, norm-referenced tests and Piagetian tests. Therefore these will be considered first and then alternative approaches will be examined.

Checklists

Checklists, especially checklists which are intended to be directly related to the curriculum sequence, are probably the most commonly used method of assessing the progress of children with PMLDs (Hogg and Sebba 1986).

One problem with checklists, which becomes particularly acute in relation to pupils with PMLDs, is to do with the selection and ordering of items. Any checklist consists of a selection from a (potentially infinite) number of behaviours relevant to the area of activity and level of development under consideration; therefore, the likelihood of distortions of emphasis in the selection and ordering of items is great (Goodstein, 1982). Generalisability, (of mastery of items to mastery of the domain they represent) or what we measure, is a problem for all checklists. Usually the problem is one of how many items is enough to reliably represent the domain, and how this requirement varies between populations. Additionally, the practical limitations on the number of items in a checklist produce the result that some children with PMLDs will make little or no recorded progress over long periods. This problem has sometimes led to checklists in which ever smaller steps proliferate, as in some of adaptations of the National Curriculum for pupils with PMLDs. Thus, even if the problems of the relevance of the general curriculum sequence to individuals with PMLDs can be overcome, there remain intractable problems in finding measures of progress which are sufficiently sensitive to discern movements towards the objective which may be very small indeed.

School- or teacher-designed curriculum-related checklists are also prone to more serious problems with the selection and ordering of items which may be done without either piloting of items or any reference to a theoretical analysis of the developmental process. If items are not adequately criterion (or domain) referenced, carefully specified and sequenced, they may not record progress in a reliable way. On the other hand, such curriculum-related checklists have a definite advantage in terms of their relevance to future teaching.

Professionally produced checklists, such the Progress Assessment Charts (Gunzberg, 1966) or The Behaviour Assessment Battery (Kiernan and Jones, 1977, 1982) share with school designed instruments criterion (rather than norm) referencing (see below) and an emphasis on behaviourial specification and developmental ordering of items. With professionally produced lists, though it may be difficult to locate one that is appropriate, the items can usually be assumed to be representative of their domain and ordered according to some accepted theoretical analysis of the developmental process. However, this may be a mixed blessing, since it is well documented that the development of individuals with PMLDs is often more variable than that of individuals without disabilities. If an appropriate, professionally produced checklist can be identified it may well share the relevance to teaching of school produced lists.

A full account of both types of checklist can be found in Hogg and Raynes (1986).

Norm-referenced and developmental tests

Alternative to this curriculum-related idea of progress are attempts to measure more global development using norm-referenced tests of one kind or another.

In research papers and to some extent in psychologists' assessments, children with PMLDs are frequently described in terms of IQ scores or developmental quotients. Despite the fact that IQ tests and their downward extension into infant developmental indices essentially measure outcomes and products rather than progress, their reliability means that if a test is repeated, differences in the obtained score can in theory be attributed to improvement or deterioration in the child's functioning.

Psychometric tests

Psychometric tests consist of a number of test items administered under standardised conditions. They are intended to measure, not progress, but general levels of mental functioning. Items are selected for their scaleability (items are always passed in the same order) and reliability in indicating a child's general level of mental functioning rather than because they represent accomplishments which are important in themselves. Items are deliberately chosen to minimise the contribution of teaching to the child's performance, since the intention is to measure the child's underlying ability rather than what they are able to achieve with teaching. Especially in the early items these tests rely heavily on intact motor and sensory responses and this makes them particularly unsuitable for people with PMLDs (Switzky and Rotatori, 1981). Additionally, the strictly controlled testing conditions on which psychometric tests rely for their validity may be particularly detrimental to individuals with PMLDs. They may be especially sensitive to unfamiliar testers or testing conditions, and exhibit a highly variable test performance (Landesman Dywer and Sackett, 1978) meaning that they will not be credited with items which have to be administered and passed on a number of successive occasions for credit to be given. Additionally, the reliability and validity of psychometric tests in relation to people with PMLDs is in doubt because such individuals are deliberately excluded from standardisation samples.

Psychometric tests offer little information that is of any relevance in planning further teaching. Although they are frequently used to define individuals with profound learning difficulties over against other groups, psychometric tests offer little which is of use in the planning of teaching or the assessment of progress.

Many of the drawbacks of psychometric norm-referenced tests apply equally to norm-referenced infant developmental tests such as the Bayley Scales of Infant Development (Bayley, 1969) and the Griffiths Mental Development Scales (Griffiths, 1970) (both of which are frequently used with people with PMLDs). Like psychometric tests, they are intended neither for use with people with PMLDs nor to provide information for programme planning. Like psychometric tests, they lack sufficient sensitivity to be useful for assessing the progress of pupils with PMLDs at anything other than the most general level.

However, a number of authors have investigated the use of the Bayley Scales with people with PMLDs (Whiteley and Krenn 1986; Naglieri, 1981; Landesman-Dwyer and Sackett, 1978). Of these, Landesman-Dwyer and Sackett's study is potentially useful to the teacher. They interpret their results as suggesting that a more consistent performance across trials may indicate progress for a person with PMLDs even if there is no increase in the actual number of items passed.

Piagetian tests

By contrast with norm-referenced infant developmental indices such as the Bayley Scales, a number of studies have found evidence of the relevance to teaching of the Uzgiris and Hunt Scales of Sensorimotor Development (Uzgiris and Hunt, 1975), a test based on the Piaget's theory of cognitive development. Goldbart (this volume) argues that while there are problems with using any assessment with people with PMLDs, the Uzgiris and Hunt test is sufficiently sensitive to pick up small changes in cognitive development, and can thus be useful for planning teaching. Of course, Piagetian tests share some of the disadvantages of norm-referenced tests; in particular they too tend to rely on intact motor responses. Additionally, while Piaget's stage theory has been demonstrated to apply to people with PMLDs in general terms, account needs to be taken of their greater variability of response

(Macpherson and Butterworth, 1988) and less successful learning histories (see Goldbart and Glenn and O'Brien this volume). In particular, Macpherson and Butterworth's research demonstrates that children with severe and profound learning difficulties develop at different rates in the different areas assessed by the sub-scales of the Uzgiris and Hunt test, and this means that performance in one area cannot be predicted with any degree of certainty from performance in another area. On the other hand, versions of Piagetian tests have been produced specifically for use with people with PMLDs (Dunst, 1980) and with physical disabilities (Sharpe, 1993). Additionally the fact that they are intended for use by a familiar tester using everyday objects is a considerable advantage.

Alternative approaches to assessing progress

From this discussion of conventional methods of assessment, it seems that there are two main problems in using them with people with PMLDs: their insensitivity to small changes relevant to the final goal and their failure to take account of the limited responses and variability of behaviour of people with PMLDs. To be worthwhile, any alternative approach to assessment must take account of these problems.

Vygotskian approaches

The principles of curriculum sequencing advocated by Baumgart et al (see above) have, it seems to me, at least something in common with what Belmont (1989) describes as a Vygotskian approach to assessment. The central idea behind such an approach is, according to Belmont, the idea that learning occurs through the 'transfer of responsibility'. Learning is interpersonal. Any child (or learner) is able to do more with the assistance of a person more skilled than themselves than they are able to achieve alone. Initially, the more skilled person in a teacher-learner pair may take responsibility for reaching the current goal; learning occurs as the less skilled person takes over that responsibility. The skilled teacher performs an analysis of the task *relative* to what the pupil is able to do with and without help. This is also the essence of partial participation. By identifying the central features of any task it is possible to ensure that progress is made towards the point where a person with PMLDs takes responsibility for reaching the goal even though they may not be able to perform all the mechanics of the actions involved. For example, in order for a person with PMLDs to have responsibility for an everyday task like having dinner they need to be able to perform some crucial part of the sequence involved in getting and consuming dinner. Arguably, being able to switch on the microwave when they want to eat gives them more responsibility for task completion (and more control over their life) than being able to load the spoon. Assessment may demonstrate that the child moans when hungry; with help they are able to eat the food which is provided, but switching on the microwave can both act as a signal that they need help with eating and give them some control over the provision of food to satisfy their hunger.

Most importantly, in this approach, the child's potential for learning is not seen as fixed, but rather as shared with the teacher; a child has more potential for learning in interaction with a particularly skilled teacher than with an unskilled one. Belmont argues that the advantage of this Vygotskian form of assessment is its capability for indicating where teaching is most likely to 'pay off' at present. This sounds very positive, and the work of Gow and colleagues (Gow et al, 1990) demonstrates the efficacy of the use of these Vygotskian principles in teaching people with mild learning difficulties. However, there have been as yet no attempts to utilise a Vygotskian approach with people with PMLDs, so its utility for this group is unproven.

Extensions of traditional methods

The assessment of the occurrence of learning using a behavioural approach has been reviewed by a number of authors (eg Remington and Evans, 1988). Here, I wish to consider the more general application of observational techniques and experimental data collection methods to the assessment of progress in children with PMLDs. The comprehensive range of data recording techniques associated with behaviourial teaching methods could be said in themselves to amount to an alternative approach to measuring progress, in the sense that finer gradation of observation and performance data enables progress to be *identified* where none can be identified using other methods. This addresses one of the major issues we identified earlier, the inability of many assessments to take account of extremely small changes in a child's performance. Research evidence indicates that greater progress has been made by children with learning difficulties when instructional decisions based on explicit, systematic data evaluation rules were used (Fuchs and Fuchs, 1986) and data graphed (Utley et al, 1987). Although this research was carried out with teachers who worked with children with less severe learning difficulties than those with PMLDs, there seems to be no reason why it should not be applicable to this group. Indeed, in our research in classrooms for pupils with PMLDs (see Chapter 7) we have found that staff appreciate the use of graphed data to demonstrate children's performance.

Specific approaches to measuring progress which depend on very detailed observation include measures of overall rates of behaviour and of the complexity of behaviour. Both these measures rely, not just on the ability to conduct observations in minute detail, but on the hypothesis that changes in them relate to development. Thus in some ways they are closely related to more conventional assessments. The idea of using behavioural complexity to measure the progress of people with PMLDs was introduced by Landesman-Dwyer and Sackett (1978) and can be defined as the range of *different* behaviours occurring within a specified time interval (calculated as the ratio of different behaviours to the total number of behaviours). The idea of increasing complexity as indicating progress is familiar from the field of biology; but its usefulness in guiding teaching and its relationship to ideas such as quality of life are unclear. From the uses of this measure in the literature (Landesman-Dwyer and Sackett, 1978; La Mendola, Zaharia and O'Brien, 1987) it is clear that its application is extremely time-consuming and requires highly trained observers so that its practicality for classroom use is very doubtful. However, the wider the range of behaviours which can be discriminated, the greater potential for understanding the person's behaviour. For example, Goldbart (this volume) uses detailed observations of behaviour in her communication assessment; and this demonstrates that clearly detailed observation can provide relevant guidance for teaching.

Observational methods have also frequently been used to measure *engagement* – the extent to which a person is involved in purposeful activity. Although the definition of purposeful activity is fraught with difficulties, especially where people with PMLDs are concerned, engagement has been shown to relate to other more conventional methods of assessing developmental level; we might therefore expect increases in engagement to be indicative of progress. However, engagement is potentially much more useful for judging the quality and appropriateness of an environment than for guiding intervention.

Non-traditional methods

One potentially useful method of assessing progress in pupils with very profound learning difficulties which has been used by several researchers is by reference to the concept of biobehavioural state (Landesman-Dwyer and Sackett, 1978; Rainforth, 1982; Guess et al,

1988: Sternberg and Richards, 1989). Biobehavioural state refers to the range of alertness between deep sleep and alert wakefulness. It is known that young infants display more rapid cycles between these states than older children and mature adults. Researchers have suggested that people with PMLDs may resemble young infants, in terms of rapidity of cycle between the various states (ie they are likely to be awake and asleep several times during the course of a day); however this has yet to be demonstrated. In terms of the conceptualisation of progress, however, the assessment of change in the relative proportions of different biobehavioural states, in the direction of increased wakefulness and alertness for example, may well be a useful way of characterising progress in children whose behavioural rates and repertoires are so limited that they preclude more conventional assessments.

Implications for conceptualising progress

One major implication of the research on assessing progress in people with PMLDs is that progress is to some extent in the eye of the beholder. New information about the detailed course of development, and microanalytic methods which enable us to see progress where before it was invisible both illustrate this point. This phenomenon suggests that an important feature of effective methods of assessing progress in children with PMLDs is the extent to which they sensitize us to positive changes in the child. Additionally this sensitization can help us target our teaching effectively by starting precisely where the child is and thus facilitate further progress. This is turn implies that failure to detect such positive changes ought to lead us, not to the conclusion that a particular child is ineducable, but rather that more sensitive assessment instruments are required.

A second major implication of examining both traditional and non-traditional methods of assessing progress in people with PMLDS is that in general they relate poorly to concepts such as quality of life. In this regard, observational assessments which aid teachers in interpreting the child's behaviour, and Vygotskian or Piagetian approaches which enable an assessment to be made of the person's degree of control over their own environment appear to offer most promise.

How we conceptualise progress is inevitably relative to both our personal values and the society in which we live. Possibly this indicates that for person with PMLDs, as for any other person, we need to attempt to see progress from their perspective. Assessment instruments should be evaluated according to the extent that they which enable us to do this and suggest ways in which we can help the individual move in the desired direction.

Acknowledgement

Some of the ideas in this chapter were first proposed by Ian Healey during discussions which took place during the Contingency-Sensitive Environments and Profoundly Handicapped Children Research Project funded by the ESRC under grant no R000 23 1239.

CHAPTER TWO

Opening the Communication Curriculum to Students with PMLDs

Juliet Goldbart

The aims of this chapter are twofold, first to identify a working definition of communication which is relevant to pupils with PMLD; and second, by using research on the development of communication in babies and in children with severe and profound learning difficulties, to work towards a communicative curriculum: specifically ways of assessing and developing communicative skills in pupils with PMLD. The most recent account of the communication skills of this group comes from Evans and Ware's (1987) survey of Special Care Units in the South East of England. (See below).

Of the 800 children on whom information is available, teachers report that 647, that is 80.9 per cent, have no communication skills.

Communication Skills: Mode of Communication used by SCU Children

	N	%
Does not communicate	647	80.9
Uses speech	123	15.4
Uses speech and signs	5	0.6
Uses signs or symbols	21	2.6
Idiosyncratic	4	0.5
Total	800	

(adapted from Evans and Ware, 1987)[1]

Of course the way that teachers have answered this question depends very much on their definition of communication. However, in many

---

1 It is interesting to note that broadly similar findings emerge from Hogg, Lambe, Cowie and Coxon's (1987) survey. In this study parents reported on their children's vocal and non-vocal communication according to an 8 and 5 point scale respectively. A little under 20 per cent of parents report their school-age sons and daughters are using spoken words for communication, although some 40 per cent suggest that their school-age children have *some* non-vocal strategy for indicating that they want a particular object.

respects, whether these teachers are right or not about their pupils' communication skills is not important. What is important is that they think of these 647 students as non-communicators. For it is well established in the language acquisition literature that it is by being treated as communicators that we become communicators.

As Newson (1978) says

> It is only because he [the child] is treated as a communicator that he learns the essential art of communication.
>
> (Newson, 1978 p. 42)

In order to tackle this problem, (and problem it is, for how are these 647 students and others like them to make progress in communication if they are never treated as communicators?) we must try to redefine communication.

Let us consider one definition, that of Sugarman (1984), 'Communication involves the *intention* to convey an idea to someone else', (p. 27, her italics). Essential for Sugarman and others (eg Owens, 1988 p. 450) is the idea that communication is something a person does knowingly; on purpose and for a purpose. In contrast we can view communication in a less restrictive way as including both communication on purpose *and* those actions and responses we make which can be interpreted by other people but which were not made *in order to* affect others.

Ellis and Beattie (1986), for example, use a definition which can apply to both human and animal communication:

> Communication occurs when one organism (the transmitter) encodes information into a signal which passes to another organism (the receiver) which decodes the signal and is capable of responding appropriately. (p. 3)

They add

> nothing in our approach to communication requires that the transmitter and/or receiver be *necessarily* aware of the fact that communication has happened . . .
>
> p. 8 (their italics)

So, we can expand our definition to include unintentional communication, or, for our purposes, *preintentional* communication. This is the information that caregivers, teachers and others can decode from the behaviour of people not yet intentionally sending messages.

This preintentional stage can be readily distinguished from the intentional stage. In the former the child's motor acts on people and objects are 'assigned communicative significance by others' (McLean and Snyder-McLean 1987). Whereas the intentionally communicating child deliberately uses particular signals with the intention of having a predetermined effect on another person (Bates et al, 1979; Wetherby et al, 1988).

Many students with PMLD will make very slow progress through the preintentional stage. Since there are clear cognitive and other developments within the stage, McLean and Snyder-McLean (1987) have subdivided it into a **Reactive Perlocutionary** stage (clients' reactive responses to internal and external stimuli serve as signals to others who assign communicative significance to these acts) and a **Proactive Perlocutionary** stage (clients' goal-oriented ie intentional motor acts on objects and/or people serve as signals to others who assign communicative intents to them).

As a result of experience with individuals functioning at a very early cognitive level (predominantly Piaget's sensorimotor substage 1) I would suggest that the Reactive stage be further subdivided into a Reflexive Perlocutionary stage (clients' reflex and very early responses to internal and external stimuli serve as signals to familiar adults who interpret them) and a Reactive stage as above (Coupe and Goldbart, 1988).

Subdivisions of Preintentional Communication

- **Reflexive Stage** – students' reflex and very early responses to internal and external stimuli serve as signals to familiar people who interpret them.

  Eg: recognising different cries as resulting from hunger, discomfort and tiredness, or interpreting a relaxed state as comfort and contentment.
- **Reactive Stage** – students' reactive responses to internal and external stimuli serve as signals to others who assign communicative significance to them.

  Eg: understanding smiling and arm waving as conveying pleasure or a stiffening of the body as conveying dislike of an event.
- **Proactive Stage** – students' goal-oriented (ie intentional) acts on objects and/or people serve as signals to others who assign communicative intent to them.

  Eg: responding to vocalisation and jigging up and down as if they were signals for 'I want that' or pursing lips and turning away as 'I don't like that'.

This continuum (see below, Table 2.1) goes some way towards providing a framework for teachers and others to view pupils as communicators.

Table 2.1: Continuum of Early Communication

REFLEXIVE		
	REACTIVE	
		PROACTIVE
PREINTENTIONAL COMMUNICATION		INTENTIONAL COMMUNICATION

This, of course, brings us to the main purpose of this chapter. For it would be grossly unfair to criticise teachers for their perception of their students without offering a structure and materials for assessment and intervention at preintentional stages. In order to provide more than the descriptive framework outlined above, my colleagues and I have looked at what research tells us about this early stage of communication, both in normally developing infants and in people with profound learning difficulties. We have tried to use this information, and existing and new assessments, to form the basis of a communication curriculum.

Harding (1983) provides us with a useful starting point by stating that the development of intentional communication appears to be a gradual process, related to both cognitive ability and social experience. Thus we have two angles to examine, both involving a look at infant development.

By suggesting that we look at how babies communicate I am not trying to say that children or young people with PMLD are like babies. A sixteen year old with PMLD has a sixteen year social history. He or she will have met a large number of people and had quite a diverse range of social experiences. But his or her learning history might have been rather unsuccessful, unlike that of the baby who has probably met only a small number of people but had a highly successful learning history.

So the baby and the sixteen year old are not the same. But, by looking in detail at the way that the baby is learning cognitive and communication skills, I would argue that we can recognise and value small changes in the development of people with PMLD and, perhaps, understand some of the processes by which they come about. This information should help us plan further small steps for teaching or therapy.

Taking cognitive development first, we can examine the learner's level of cognitive functioning across different domains. To do this I have found Piaget's (eg 1952) account of infant development useful. Table

2.2 presents my interpretation of some aspects of Piaget's account of infant development.

Table 2.2: Cognitive development in the sensory motor period

Sub Stage	Age	Label	Description
1	0–6 weeks	Reflex	Engages mainly in exercise of reflexes eg sucking, rooting. Some selective looking. Change in activity level on seeing a visually presented object.
2	6 weeks–4 months	Primary Circular Reactions	If infant does something with her own body that she finds pleasurable, eg sucks her thumb, she learns to repeat the action. Undifferentiated schemes eg looking, holding, mouthing.
3	4–8 months	Secondary Circular Reactions	If infant does something external to himself by chance, eg makes a mobile swing, he learns to repeat the action. Therefore first stage of intentionality. Differentiated schemes eg tearing, sliding.
4	8–12 months	Coordination of Secondary Schemes	Establishes goal prior to initiation of activity therefore intentionality fully established. Infant can coordinate previously unrelated actions to produce interesting results or solve simple problems. Functional use of objects eg cup, shoe.
5	12–18 months	Tertiary Circular Reactions	New means of achieving ends through experimentation. Exploration of container-contents relationships. Showing and giving objects. Relational then self-pretend play.
6	18–24 months	Beginnings of Thought	New means of achieving ends through mental combinations. Predicts cause-effect relationships. Decentred then sequenced pretend play.

Ages are approximate but the sequence is invariant.

Adapted from Piaget (eg 1952), Uzgiris and Hunt (1975) and Dunst (1980).

There are three areas of particular importance. The first concerns increasing sophistication in relating to objects. At these early stages 'schemes' or 'schemata' can be seen as typical ways of responding to objects. There are important developmental changes here from the very early (substages 1-2) undifferentiated responses (everything is held and/or looked at and/or sucked) to actions which show that the infant is responding to the physical properties of the objects. For example a rattle is interesting to bang and slide on a surface but cannot be pulled apart or squashed. Cotton wool, however, is very boring to bang but can be pulled into little pieces and squashed. Later (substage 4 onwards) babies start to demonstrate that they are aware of the social or functional uses of objects. Usually the earliest way they show this is by picking up a cup presented in any orientation and starting to drink out of it.

These developments in relating to objects are obviously important for communication as we cannot expect the child to learn the names of objects without some understanding of what objects are for and how they differ. This poses problems for teachers of pupils with severe sensory and physical impairments who will have to plan carefully to ensure access to and experience of a diversity of objects.

The second important issue concerns the infant's increasing understanding of how to make things happen. During substage 2 the infant learns that she can repeat actions involving her own body. If, for example, she gets her thumb in her mouth and likes the feeling, she learns at first to maintain the action, that is to keep her thumb in her mouth. Then she learns how to get her thumb into her mouth, ie, to repeat the action. Piaget called these actions on self 'Primary Circular Reactions'.

During the next substage (substage 3) the infant learns to continue and then to repeat actions *external* to his own body. This presumably comes about by repeated chance experience. For example: the baby is lying in his pram. When he kicks his legs in the air they hit the row of plastic elephants strung across the pram. The elephants bounce up and down and rattle. After several chance repetitions of the event the baby makes the connection between his action and the consequence. He realises he can make things happen. This realisation that you can have an effect on the world is called 'intentionality'. Babies typically show that they have grasped the beginning of this idea at around six months.

Intentionality is likely to be crucial for developing intentional communication as, until you realise you can affect the environment (*intentionality*), you are not going to realise that you can specifically affect the behaviour of people in the environment (*intentional communication*).

This issue is important for another reason which, though not central to this chapter, is important enough to justify a small digression. Many children with PMLD have sensory and or motor impairments in addition to their learning difficulties. It may, therefore, be far more difficult for them to act on the environment in the way described above. Even if they do, their visual or auditory impairments restrict the amount of feedback they get from their actions. This may prevent them making the transition from primary to secondary circular reactions.

All organisms need to maintain a certain level of arousal in order to stay conscious. Receiving changing sensory input is one of the ways in which an acceptable level of arousal or alertness is maintained. If we are very bored or tired we all have strategies to keep ourselves awake; fiddling with our hair, doodling, eating and so on. People with PMLD who have not acquired secondary circular reactions do not have recourse to such external actions to maintain arousal. They are likely, therefore, to use primary circular reactions. These actions on self may become quite extreme, especially if the person has reduced access to sensory stimulation, and become self stimulatory stereotyped behaviours such as hand biting, eye poking or head banging, all of which may be 'preferable' to sensory deprivation. Once these behaviours are a common part of an individual's behavioural repertoire they may prevent more useful behaviours being learned and the child may become 'stuck' at this stage of primary circular reactions.

All these aspects suggest that assessing cognitive development in pupils with PMLD may be useful. A method for carrying out such an assessment is Uzgiris and Hunt's (1975) Ordinal Scales of Psychological Development.

For anyone unfamiliar with this assessment, it is comprised of six scales, based on Piaget's account (eg 1952) of sensorimotor intelligence. They cover visual pursuit and object permanence, means of obtaining desired environmental ends, gestural and vocal imitation, construction of object relations in space, operational causality and object related schemes, as shown below:

Summary of the six sub-scales

1. **The Development of Visual Pursuit and the Permanence of Objects**
   Fixating on and tracking objects, recognising the continued existence of partially hidden and hidden objects, retrieving partially hidden and hidden objects.
2. **Means of Obtaining Desired Environmental Events**
   Increasingly complex ways of making things happen. Getting repetition, various ways of getting objects, strategic planning for achieving ends.
3. **The development of a) Vocal Imitation and b) Gestural Imitation**

a) Differentiated coos and distress sounds, imitation of sounds already in repertoire, imitates some new sounds, will imitate most sounds.
b) Imitates familiar own-body actions, imitates visible gestures, imitates invisible gestures, imitates new models of gestures.

4. **The Development of Operational Causality**
Increasing levels of understanding of what makes events happen. (Some overlap with scale 2.) Profound egocentricity, self at centre of all events, self and others make things happen.

5. **Construction of Object Relations in Space**
Increasingly complex understanding of spatial relations. Tracking, grasping, appreciation of spatial effects eg gravity, and position of objects.

6. **The Development of Schemes Relating to Objects**
Reflexes, simple undifferentiated schemes, differentiated schemes, dropping and throwing objects, socially instigated schemes.

Adapted from Uzgiris and Hunt (1975) *Assessment in Infancy*, University of Illinois Press.

Whilst this assessment was originally standardised on normally developing infants, Kahn (1976) demonstrated that its use with children with severe and profound learning difficulties is both reliable and valid. To facilitate the use of the scales with such children Dunst (1980) has developed a more detailed and practical manual and scoring system. I have seen both Uzgiris and Hunt's original scales and Dunst's adaptation used successfully in schools in the UK.

There are, of course, problems in assessing children with multiple learning difficulties by any means, and the Uzgiris and Hunt Scales are not a perfect solution. But they do offer a valuable, sensitive measure of sensorimotor development across the six domains.

One study which has looked at the relationship between cognition and communication in pupils with severe and profound learning difficulties, using Uzgiris and Hunt's scales, was carried out by Mundy, Seibert and Hogan (1984). When they studied children at similar cognitive levels to those studied in research, (eg by Bates et al 1979), on normally developing infants (8–13 months), Mundy et al found that the children's performance on the 'means-ends' and 'object-related schemes' scales tied in closely with their levels of communication skills. These two cognitive domains are two which have been found to be important by Bates et al and others.

However, with children at lower developmental levels (2–7 months) who would be at preintentional stages of communication, Mundy et al found relationships between cognition in a wider range of domains: 'means-end', 'object-related schemes', 'object permanence', 'causality' and, to a lesser extent, 'object relations in space'.

Because these are only correlational data they do not prove that teaching cognition (assuming that this can be done) would help the student develop their communicative skills. However, there are a number of studies which have successfully tested this idea (eg Harrison, Lombardino and Stapell, 1987; Kahn, 1984, and Schweigert 1989).

For example Schweigert argues forcibly that without contingency awareness, the realisation that actions have consequences, the child cannot learn to engage in intentional communication. In support of this view, he has demonstrated the effectiveness of teaching contingency awareness of a social nature, using microswitch technology, to a child with PMLD. The child progressed to using this microswitch system for simple communication.

The use of microtechnology has opened up great possibilities for the teacher or therapist working with children with PMLD (see Glenn and O'Brien, chapter 5). This is primarily because it enables the activation of highly salient consequences contingent on the emission of very subtle behaviours. Hence, we can give children with very little voluntary movement experience of controlling their environment. Because of the parallel between this experience and Piaget's Secondary Circular Reactions (eg Piaget, 1952), and the role these play in the normally developing infant's progression towards intentional communication, I would support the devising of individual programmes based on the use of microtechnology to teach contingency awareness and intentionality.

As another example, Kahn (1984) has demonstrated the effectiveness of prior cognitive training in either the object permanence or the means-ends domain on subsequent communication training. This was in a two year intervention programme with 3–10 year old children with PMLD.

Thus one intervention route teachers can follow is to work on early cognitive development, informed by, for example, Uzgiris and Hunt's assessment. In children with very little voluntary movement this could be by means of microtechnology.

Tables 2.3a and 2.3b, and 2.4a and 2.4b present cognitive assessment data for two pupils, Asif and Anna, from Dunst's adaptation of Uzgiris and Hunt's scales.

Asif has major visual and physical difficulties which compound his cognitive impairments. As ACA data presented later in this chapter indicate, he seems to dislike the sensation of touching some objects. He does not appear to be able to bring his hands to his mouth or have many

Table 2.3a: Development of means for obtaining desired environmental events
Child's name: Asif

SCALE STEP	AGE PLACEMENT (MONTHS)	DEVELOPMENTAL STAGE	ELICITING CONTEXT	CRITICAL ACTION CODE	CRITICAL BEHAVIOURS
E_8 △	2	I	Visual Awareness		Activity level increases or decreases on seeing a visual presented object *for auditory or olfactory presentation only*
1	2	II	Hand Watching	1b	Child engages in hand watching
2	3	III	Secondary Circular Reaction	3c	Repeats arm movements to keep a toy activated
3	4	III	Visually Directed Reaching	2b	Visually directed reaching hand and object both in view
4	5	III	Visually Directed Reaching	2c	Visually directed reaching brings closed hand up to object
E_9	5	III	Visually Directed Reaching	2d	Visually directed reaching shapes hand in anticipation of securing object
5	7	IV	Multiple Objects	4c	Drops one or both objects held in hands to obtain a third object
E_{10}	8	IV	Barrier		Pushes obstruction (e.g. pillow or Plexiglas) out of the way to obtain an object
6	8	IV	Support	6d 6c	Pulls support to obtain an object placed on it
7	9	IV	Locomotion	5c	Uses some form of locomotion as a means to obtain an out of reach object
8	10	V	Support	7c	Does not pull support with object held above it
E_{11}	10	V	Support		Does not pull either of two supports with object placed between them
9	11	V	String (horizontal)	8c 8d	Pull string along a horizontal surface to obtain an object attached to it
E_{12}	12	V	String (horizontal)		Pulls the correct one of two strings to obtain an object attached to one string

10	13	V	String (vertical)	9c 9f	Uses string vertically pulls object up from floor
E_{13}	18	V	T-Stick		Uses T-stick as a tool to obtain an out of reach object
11	19	V	Stick	10d 10e	Uses a stick as a tool to obtain an out of reach object
E_{14}	19	V	Matchbox		Opens and removes the contents of a small matchbox
E_{15}	19	V	Necklace (container)	11d	Invents method to place the necklace into the container
E_{16}	19	V	Solid Ring	12c	Solid ring attempts to stack avoids subsequently
12	20	VI	Necklace (container)	11e	Shows foresight in placing the necklace into the container
E_{17}	20	VI	Matchbox		Shows foresight in placing a chain into a matchbox
13	24	VI	Solid Ring	12d	Shows foresight by not stacking the solid ring
E_{18}	24	VI	Tube (Clear)		Uses stick to push out a toy inserted in a clear tube
E_{19}	26	VI	Tube (Opaque)		Uses stick to push out a toy inserted in an opaque tube

△ = qualified success on this item; italics = assessor's comment. From Dunst, 1980.

Table 2.3b: Development of schemes for relating to objects
Child's name: Asif

SCALE STEP	AGE PLACEMENT (MONTHS)	DEVELOPMENTAL STAGE	ELICITING CONTEXT	CRITICAL ACTION CODE	CRITICAL BEHAVIOURS
E_{48} ▲	1	I	Grasping Reaction	-	Grasps examiner's finger
E_{49} △	2	II	Retention of Objects	a	Retains object placed in hands for 10 to 15 seconds *for very few items*
1	3	II	Mouthing	b	Mouths objects placed in the hand *cannot bring hands to mouth*
2	3	II	Visual Inspection	c	Visually inspects objects held in the hands
3	5	III	Simple Schemes	d1	Uses simple motor schemes (banging or hitting objects on a table surface)
4	6	III	Simple Schemes	d2	Uses simple motor schemes (shaking, waving, etc.) independent of hitting a surface
E_{50}	7	III	Letting Go	-	Drops or throws objects – no visual monitoring of action
5	7	III	Examining	e	Rotates objects, examining the various sides
6	9	IV	Complex Actions	f	Uses complex motor schemes (slides, crumples, swings, tears, etc.)
7	10	IV	Letting Go	g	Drops or throw objects – visual monitoring of results of action/terminal location of object

△ = qualified success on this item; ▲ = success on this item; italics = comment. From Dunst, 1980.

other voluntary hand or arm movements. He does, however, have some voluntary head movement. He is currently gaining experience of making things happen by learning to use a broken beam switch to switch on a tape recorder.

Anna has severe nystagmus but otherwise much useful vision. She has quite good hand control, but her actions with objects tend to be rather stereotyped. Anna will work for quite long periods of time using a single switch to get a flashing light display and/or to hear certain types of music. Hence she is now clearly showing intentionality.

A second fruitful area of research also involves normally developing infants, in this case in interaction with their caregivers. In a study referred to earlier, Harding (1983) describes the progression of normally developing infants towards intentional communication:

Mother – infant interactions and the development of communication

Birth to 6 months – Phase 1

Baby's behaviours eg kicking, crying, cooing are not yet intentional.	Mother attributes meaning but not intent to these behaviours.

6 months to 8 months – Phase 2

Baby's behaviours are clearly goal-directed (ie intentional). Baby's vocalisations, looking and gestures are significant for mother.	Mother attributes **intent** as well as **meaning**, ie treats baby as an intentional communicator, and ensures baby achieves goal.

8 months

Baby has learned that 'a mutual means of communication exists'.

I am afraid that only mothers were included in Harding's study.

Table 2.4a: Development of means for obtaining desired environmental events
Child's name: Anna

SCALE STEP	AGE PLACEMENT (MONTHS)	DEVELOPMENTAL STAGE	ELICITING CONTEXT	CRITICAL ACTION CODE	CRITICAL BEHAVIOURS
E_8	2	I	Visual Awareness	-	Activity level increases or decreases on seeing a visually presented object
1	2	II	Hand Watching	1b	Child engages in hand watching
2 ▲	3	III	Secondary Circular Reaction	3c	Repeats arm movements to keep a toy activated
3 ▲	4	III	Visually Directed Reaching	2b	Visually directed reaching hand and object both in view
4 ▲	5	III	Visually Directed Reaching	2c	Visually directed reaching brings closed hand up to object
E_9 ▲	5	III	Visually Directed Reaching	2d	Visually directed reaching shapes hand in anticipation of securing object
5 ▲	7	IV	Multiple Objects	4c	Drops one or both objects held in hands to obtain a third object
E_{10}	8	IV	Barrier		Pushes obstruction (e.g., pillow or Plexiglas) out of the way to obtain an object
6	8	IV	Support	6d 6c	Pulls support to obtain an object placed on it
7 ▲	9	IV	Locomotion	5c	Uses some form of locomotion as a means to obtain an out of reach object
8	10	V	Support	7c	Does not pull support with object held above it
E_{11}	10	V	Support		Does not pull either of two supports with object placed between them
9	11	V	String (horizontal)	8c 8d	Pulls string along a horizontal surface to obtain an object attached to it

E_{12}	12	V	String (horizontal)		Pulls the correct one of two strings to obtain an object attached to one string
10	13	V	String (vertical)	9e 9f	Uses string vertically pulls object up from floor
E_{13}	18	V	T-Stick		Uses T-stick as a tool to obtain an out of reach object
11	19	V	Stick	10d 10c	Uses a stick as a tool to obtain an out of reach object
E_{14}	19	V	Matchbox		Opens and removes the contents of a small matchbox
E_{15}	19	V	Necklace (container)	11d	Invents method to place the necklace into the container
E_{16}	19	V	Solid Ring	12c	Solid ring attempts to stack avoids subsequently
12	20	VI	Necklace (container)	11e	Shows foresight in placing the necklace into the container
E_{17}	20	VI	Matchbox		Shows foresight in placing a chain into a matchbox
13	24	VI	Solid Ring	12d	Shows foresight by not stacking the solid ring
E_{18}	24	VI	Tube (clear)		Uses stick to push out a toy inserted in a clear tube
E_{19}	26	VI	Tube (opaque)		Uses stick to push out a toy inserted in an opaque tube

▲ = Behaviours that Anna can and will show on occasion; their reliability is limited by her apparent lack of interest in objects. From Dunst, 1980.

Table 2.4b: Development of schemes for relating to objects
Child's name: Anna Date of birth: .... Date of test: ....

SCALE STEP	AGE PLACEMENT (MONTHS)	DEVELOPMENTAL STAGE	ELICITING CONTEXT	CRITICAL ACTION CODE	CRITICAL BEHAVIOURS	COMMENTS
E_{48} ▲	21	I	Grasping Reaction	-	Grasp's examiner's finger	
E_{49} ▲	2	II	Retention of Objects	a	Retains object placed in hands for 10 to 15 seconds	*If she can put in mouth*
1 ▲	3	II	Mouthing	b	Mouths objects placed in the hand	
2 ▲	3	II	Visual Inspection	c	Visually inspects objects held in the hands	
3 ▲	5	III	Simple Schemes	1d	Uses simple motor schemes (banging or hitting objects on a table surface)	*Rather stereotyped actions*
4 ▲	6	III	Simple Schemes	2d	Uses simple motor schemes (shaking, waving, etc.)	
E_{50} ▲	7	III	Letting Go	-	Drops or throws objects – no visual monitoring of action	
5	7	III	Examining	e	Rotates objects, examining the various sides	
6	9	IV	Complex Actions	f	Uses complex motor schemes (slides, crumples, swings, tears, etc.)	
7	10	IV	Letting Go	g	Drops or throws objects – visual monitoring of results of action/terminal location of object.	
E_{51}	11	IV	Social Actions	h	Socially instigated actions – self and/or others	
8	13	V	Social Actions	h	Socially instigated actions – inanimate objects	

E_{52}	14	V	Giving	-	Gives object to another person to instigate social interaction	
9	15	V	Showing	i	Shows objects (does not give) to others	
10	19	VI	Naming	j	Spontaneously names objects, persons, actions, etc.	
E_{53}	24	VI	Symbolic Play	-	Symbolic play – uses one object as a signifier for another object (e.g., a stick for a spoon)	

▲ = Behaviours Anna will show if the object interests her. From Dunst, 1980.

However, there seems to be no reason why the findings should not be related to fathers too.

In the first few months of life, the baby's behaviours, such as kicking, crying, cooing, which are not as yet goal-directed, have an effect on the mother's behaviour. Thus 'the mother attributes meaning but not intent to a very wide diversity of her baby's actions'.

As infants progress cognitively, their behaviour becomes more focused, until at around six months it is starting to be goal-directed or intentional (Harding, 1982). From this point mothers generally act as though their babies are intentionally communicating. They focus primarily on responding to the babies' vocalisations, looking and gestures, thus ensuring that their infants achieve their goals. Through this systematic feedback infants learn 'that a mutual means of communication exists' (Harding 1983, p. 111). We might even say that mothers are *shaping* intentional communication.

This gives us two important areas to follow-up. One, the role of caregiver-child interactions, I will come on to later. The other concerns the selectiveness of mothers' responding.

It is clear from Harding's (1983) work that mothers infer communicative intent from vocalisation, looking and gestures, and not from more global body movements. Students with PMLD may be seriously disadvantaged in this respect; visual impairments, prevalent in people with PMLD (Hogg and Sebba, 1986), will affect the child's ability to control and direct their looking from object to person. Motor difficulties, such as cerebral palsy may severely restrict the child's ability to gesture and also their ability to coordinate breathing and making sounds in order to vocalise. Auditory impairments, again often a feature of PMLD (Hogg and Sebba, 1986), will affect feedback from vocalisation.

Teachers and parents, however, will know that children with PMLD respond with more idiosyncratic actions to events, experiences etc. In my experience (eg Goldbart, Warner and Mount, 1994) parents especially can be particularly skilful in interpreting such responses, generally at the 'gut-reaction' level. One approach which aims to enable teachers and others to formalise and make sense of these gut-reactions is the Affective Communication Assessment (ACA) devised by Coupe and colleagues (Coupe, Barton, Barber, Collins, Levy and Murphy 1985). (See Table 2.5).

This is a content-free assessment. To complete it, the child is presented, at intervals, with stimuli or experiences that seem likely to elicit strong responses. Each response is interpreted by people who know the child well, (we have found the involvement of parents invaluable

Table 2.5: ACA observation and recording sheet

ACA OBSERVATION Recording Sheet	STIMULI								DATE:		
CHILD'S NAME:											
HEAD											
Turn Left/Right Up/Down											
Activity ↑ ↓											
Rotating											
Other											
FACE											
Rotating											
Smile											
Anguish											
MOUTH											
Activity ↑ ↓											
Open/close											
Tongue activity ↑ ↓											
Contact											
EYES											
Activity ↑ ↓											
Open/close											
Gaze											
Localise/search											
HANDS											
Activity ↑ ↓											
Finger activity ↑ ↓											
Contact											
ARMS											
Reaching											
Activity ↑ ↓											
LEGS											
Activity ↑ ↓											
BODY											
Activity ↑ ↓											
VOCALISATION											
Utterance											
Cry											
Laugh											
OTHER											
AFFECTIVE COMMUNICATION Interpretation of child's behaviour											

Table 2.6: Completed ACA observation sheet: Asif

ACA OBSERVATION Recording sheet	STIMULI					DATE: 16 years		
CHILD'S NAME: Asif	"Babyliss" Massager on hands	Perfume (smell of) in mouth	Plum jam in mouth	Lemon juice	Music M. Jackson	Coriander (smell of)	Foil in hands	put in bath of warm water
HEAD Turn Left/Right Up/Down Activity ↑ ↓ Rotating Other	↓	Down a bit-see "other" ↓		↑	✓ Turns to source R and L	Down a bit see "other" ↓	↑	↑
FACE Frown Smile Anguish				✓			?✓	✓
MOUTH Activity ↑ ↓ Open/close Tongue activity ↑ ↓ Contact	↑		↑	↑ O ↑	↑↑	↑ lips ✓		
EYES Activity ↑ ↓ Open/close Gaze Localise/search	O↑ widen	O↑ widen ✓		O-& C	O↑ widen ✓	O↑ widen		
HANDS Activity ↑ ↓ Finger activity ↑ ↓ Contact	↑? seems to try to keep contact	↑L	↑?	↑?	↑		↑ ↑ seems to try to avoid contact	

ARMS Reaching activity ↑ ↓				↑			↑■	↑
LEGS Activity ↑ ↓				↑ slight				↑
BODY Activity ↑ ↓	↓	↓			↓	↓		↑
VOCALISATION Utterance Cry Laugh								
OTHER		Seems to keep nose over bottle				seems to keep nose over packet		
AFFECTIVE COMMUNICATION Interpretation of child's behaviour	Aware of__ likes?	Aware of__ likes	Aware of__ neutral?	Strong dislike but some res- ponses may be reflex- ive	Aware of__ likes?	Likes	Aware of dislikes?	Dislikes

■ Swings Lower arm over back of chair ↑ = increases ↓ = decreases o = open c = close here). Then the components of the response are isolated and recorded so as to give a behavioural record of what the interpretation is based on. It is often useful to present the stimulus or experience twice, in order to see if the student responds in a way that can be interpreted as wanting or rejecting more of the experience. The extent to which the student is acting on the environment in this way gives valuable data on whether he or she is at the reactive or proactive preintentional stage as outlined above (McLean and Snyder-McLean 1987).

Typical, and useful, interpretations that we have found (eg Coupe, Barber and Murphy, 1988) are *like* and *strong like*, *dislike* and *strong dislike*, *wants*, or *rejects*, *more*, *puzzled*, and *aware but neutral*. We can now examine two examples of completed ACA Observation Sheets (Tables 2.6 and 2.7). They are for Asif and Anna whose cognitive assessment data were presented earlier.

Having obtained these data, we can now look for typical patterns. Typical, that is, for the individual concerned, for they may well be very different from the vocalisation, looking and reaching pattern identified by Harding (1983). We can see from Asif's ACA data (Table 2.6) that observers have been cautious in interpreting his responses to some stimuli. The responses he does make are often slight and many involve a decrease in activity from his usual rocking pattern. However, we can interpret a range of responses from *dislike* through *neutral* to *like*.

The next stage in using the assessment is to look for any clusters of behaviours which seem to be fairly regularly associated with a particular response. For example, in Asif's case, a decrease in body activity, eye widening and a decrease in head activity seem to be indicators of *like*. We would not expect these responses to be completely consistent and some would only be associated with, for example, food and drink stimuli. However, it should be possible to identify some likely behaviours or patterns of behaviour which are worth testing further.

These behaviours are then listed in the left hand column of the second ACA sheet; the assessment sheet (see Tables 2.8 and 2.9). It may be useful to group them according to your interpretation as I have done for Asif and Anna. For Asif, the first five responses have all been associated with *like* interpretations, the next eight with *dislike* and the final four do not fit a clear pattern.

The next stage of the ACA procedure is to present another range of experiences to the child, interpret their responses and check whether the behaviours you identified are again fairly regularly associated with a particular interpretation. In other words, has your hypothesis held up? In Asif's second set of data, we can see a reasonable consistency with two or three of a set of five behaviours being associated with each *like* response and some pattern holding with his *dislike* responses. We would want more data to be completely sure, but there is sufficient here for us to start using Asif's own responses to influence our interactions with him.

Clearly Asif is not yet at a six month developmental level and adults working with him still need to be very rich, facilitative interpreters. However, they should be able to be more sensitive to his responses, and should be in a stronger position to shape intentional communications from Asif's idiosyncratic responses when this becomes appropriate.

Anna (Table 2.7) shows much more easily interpretable responses in which *wants* can sometimes be distinguished from *likes*. However, it is hard to find experiences she dislikes. Her class teacher (Barber, personal communication) suggests wryly that, if you are visually impaired, non-ambulant and have profound learning difficulties, perhaps any stimulation is better than none. Nevertheless, we can look through these data for typical patterns of responses which may be very individual to Anna. The positive clusters for *want*, *like* and *dislike* are presented in Table 2.9. Readers may like to consider the sort of stimuli they would use to see if these clusters of responses really are in any way consistent.

In Anna's case, since she is showing intentionality (see cognition section) we can respond to these patterns systematically; giving her things she shows us she likes, more of things we see she wants and taking away or changing things she shows she dislikes. By doing this we hope to teach Anna to communicate intentionally.

We can see that by using the data from the ACA to sensitise themselves to these idiosyncratic, but not random, responses, teachers and others can give pupils with PMLD some of the systematic feedback that seems to be teaching normally developing infants to be intentional communicators.

The definition of communication adopted in this chapter (eg Ellis and Beattie, 1986) requires that communication is seen as an activity that pervades the whole of everyday life, rather than a topic which is timetabled for 10 – 10.45 on Tuesdays and Thursdays. This reinforces the importance of involving parents in the assessment of their child's communication skills and any subsequent intervention. Parents' wish for involvement was highlighted by Hogg, Lambe, Cowie and Coxon (1987), with parents of 78 per cent of the children in their survey requesting further advice in this area.

Failure to have responses underlying *wanting*, *liking*, *disliking* and *rejecting* recognised may be further reasons why challenging behaviours may develop. On page 42 we list likely causes of stereotyped, self-injurious and other challenging behaviours.

Table 2.7: Completed ACA observation sheet: Anna

ACA OBSERVATION Recording Sheet	STIMULI							DATE: JULY-AGE13	
CHILD'S NAME: Anna	Shout her name	Play with her hair	Marmite	Whisper her name	Salad cream	Lemon juice	Flashing lights	Cola	Tickle fingers
HEAD									
Turn (Towards or away from stimulus)	To		Away		Away	To	To	To	
Activity ↑↓		↓		↓		↑			↓
Rotating									
Other							Fixates		
FACE									
Frown							✓		
Smile	✓	✓	✓			✓	✓✓	✓✓	
Anguish									
MOUTH									
Activity ↑↓		↓		↓	■	↑			✓
Open/close						O			
Tongue activity ↑↓			↑		↑			↑	
Contact			✓			✓			
EYES									
Activity ↑↓						↑	↑		
Open/close					C			C	
Gaze	✓	✓		✓		✓			✓

Localise/search	✓	✓	✓	✓		✓	✓		
HANDS									
Activity		↓	To mouth	↓		↑ To mouth ↑		↓	↓ Or claps
Finger activity									
Contact									
ARMS									
Reaching						✓	✓✓		
Activity ↑↓		↓		↓		↑			↓
LEGS					Drawn Up				
Activity ↑↓		↓	↑	↓	↑				↓
BODY									
Activity ↑↓		↓		↓					↓
VOCALISATION									
Utterance	✓✓					✓	✓✓		
Cry									
Laugh			✓		✓	✓		✓	
OTHER		*		*	■	salivation	Eats Chair		*
AFFECTIVE COMMUNICATION Interpretation of child's behaviour	V.Strong Like	Strong Want	Strongly Aware ? ?negative	Strong Want	?Dislike?	Strong Like/want	Strong Interest/ Like	Strong Like	Strong want

* = Tries to maintain contact ▼ = Curls up ■ = Regurgitates continuously ↑ = increases ↓ = decreases o = open c = closed

Table 2.8: Second ACA observation sheet: Asif

ACA IDENTIFICATION Recording Sheet	**STIMULI**								**DATE:** **AGE: 16 years**			
CHILD'S NAME: Asif	Playdough in hands	Teacher's fingers in hand	Music – Beethoven	Music – Cajun	Spiced food – smell of	Potato puree – taste	Moving him in his wheelchair					
Head activity ↓		✓										
Turning head to, or keeping head over, source			✓	✓	✓							
Eye widening					✓							
Tries to keep hand contact		✓										
Body activity ↓		✓	✓	✓	✓	✓						
Head activity ↑	✓					✓	✓					
Anguished expression	Slight											
Opens mouth												
Avoids hand contact	✓ Attempts											
Arm activity ↑	✓											

Table 2.8 continued from page 40

Big left arm movement							✓					
Leg activity ↑							✓					
Body activity ↑												
Mouth activity ↑					✓	✓						
Tongue activity ↑						✓						
Finger activity ↑	✓	gentle pressure ✓	slight ✓	slight ✓	✓	✓						
Lip movements					↑	↑						
AFFECTIVE COMMUNICATION Interpretation of child's behaviour	Mild dislike?	Likes	Aware of/Mild like?	Aware of/mild like?	Likes	Neutral or mild dislike	Dislike					

Table 2.9: Second ACA observation sheet: Anna

ACA OBSERVATION Recording sheet	STIMULI													DATE:		
CHILD'S NAME: Anna																
Head activity ↓																
Mouth activity ↓																
Hand activity ↓																
Arm activity ↓																
Leg activity ↓																
Body activity ↓																
Tries to keep contact																
Turns to stimulus																
Smiles																
Looks/Gaze																
Localise/search																
Utterance																
Laugh																

Table 2.9 continued from page 42

Turns away																
Tongue activity ↑																
Leg activity ↑																
Curls up																
AFFECTIVE COMMUNICATION Interpretation of child's behaviour																

Some causes of stereotyped, self-injurious and other challenging behaviours

1. 'Developmental' Reactions.
    - failure to establish Secondary Circular Reactions.
2. Understimulation
    - 'boredom' or 'wanting' responses and frustration not recognised or responded to.
    - Communicative intentions (eg seeking attention/sensory stimulation/positive interaction/need satisfaction) not acquired or not responded to.
3. Rejection or avoidance of stimulation or demands:
    - overarousal
    - dislike or rejection responses not recognised or responded to
    - communicative intentions (eg simple negation, rejection or denial) not acquired or not responded to.
4. Response to pain.
5. Response to extreme emotional situation, eg distress, anxiety, uncertainty or frustration.
6. Primary 'Medical' Reason, eg Lesch-Nyhan Syndrome.
7. Original reason unclear, but behaviour has become habitual.

We can see that the child whose 'bored' or 'wants' responses are not recognised may become frustrated and/or understimulated. More extreme behaviours may then substitute for the unrecognised responses, particularly if these do result in some adult response. Similarly, if we do not pick up on a child's idiosyncratic responses associated with disliking or rejecting something, someone, somewhere etc, much stronger rejecting behaviours may be used instead. If these are responded to, either because they are correctly interpreted or because doing them makes the child more likely to be left alone, they may become the child's typical way of responding. Whilst this analysis clearly holds only for some children, it does indicate a further importance of being able to interpret children's own signals.

We can now return to our third line of thinking, drawn from research on the importance of caregiver-child interactions. It has been well established, in the literature on normally developing infants, that the underpinnings of communication are learned in caregiver-child interactions (eg Bruner, 1983; Harding, 1983; Kaye, 1979; Newson, 1979; Stern, 1977).

Evans and Ware's (1987) finding that 80.9 per cent of pupils in Special Care Units are thought not to communicate might suggest that these

Units are thought not to communicate might suggest that these pupils may be experiencing rather fewer of these interactions than normally developing infants at similar stages.

Schweigert (1989) echoes this suspicion, saying

> the caregiver confronted with signals from the child that may be difficult to interpret may produce fewer and fewer responses to the child's behaviours. The prospect for developing effective communicative exchanges is bleak indeed. (p. 194)

That signals from children with severe handicaps are more difficult to interpret has been demonstrated by Paul Yoder (1987), though it should be noted that the interpretation was carried out by observers trained to use a coding scheme, not by familiar caregivers or teachers.

Certainly the frequency of adult responses to students with PMLD's initiations is very low. In my own research (Goldbart, 1985) I have found that both preschool and school age children with severe learning difficulties initiate interactions with adults less frequently and less successfully than normally developing preschoolers. Ware and Evans (1986) report that for pupils in Special Care Units 'overwhelmingly the most common response to all child initiations is a failure to respond at all'.

Disappointingly, Ware (see Chapter 8) has found that whilst training may result in teachers and assistants responding to more potentially communicative child behaviours (eg voluntary behaviours rather than sneezes) the overall frequency of their responding is not significantly increased.

Given that Stern (1977) reports normally developing infants initiating interactions by four months of age, it seems likely that adults, in this case teachers, are missing signals for initiation or failing to recognise them. Missing the signals could result from organisational factors such as staff ratios or demands on time, and failure to recognise signals might stem either from features of the children themselves or from teachers' definitions of them as non-communicators. However, the importance of interaction in the development of people with PMLD has been demonstrated very effectively in studies by Burford (eg Burford, 1988 and this volume) and Hewett and Nind, (eg Hewett, 1989; Nind, 1993).

Mindful of Harrison et al's (1987) exhortation that 'interventionists who are providing stimulation for communication must learn to recognise the child's orienting behaviours which signal a desire to initiate, maintain or terminate interactions' (p. 465), I worked with a teacher to devise an observational assessment of early interactions (Goldbart and Rigby 1989). The aim of this assessment was the identification of signals or strategies that individual pupils use to *initiate, maintain*, *terminate* and *repair* their interactions with others. The idea behind the assessment was that if we had a clear picture of how individuals were trying to engage in interaction with us, we would be more likely to respond to them.

In order to devise the assessment my colleague (a teacher) and I spent a lot of time watching interactions between pupils with PMLD and classroom staff and others. We also looked at research on interaction with young infants. From these two sources we identified likely strategies for initiating interactions, keeping them going and for terminating them, and also for repairing or restarting conversations that had stopped against the wishes of one participant (repair strategies).

We used this information to develop the protocols presented in Tables 2.10, 2.11 and 2.12 and checked that two observers could agree on how to record what they had seen. We found it easiest to use the assessment for observations recorded on video, but it was possible to record 'live' though with lower levels of inter-observer agreement.

The assessment starts with some background information and, for the sake of comparison, a statement of what the child does when not interacting with anyone. Since this assessment is not yet published elsewhere, three examples have been included so that the reader can see a range of interaction strategies. Asif and Anna have been described earlier in this chapter. Hazel is a very sociable child who would rather interact with adults than engage with any kind of objects. She sits unsupported and has no reported sensory or perceptual difficulties. She is not independently mobile but has acquired intentionality.

The interaction recorded in Table 2.10a happened during lunchtime and involved Hazel and Joyce who was feeding her. Before the interaction Joyce had turned away from Hazel to get a plate of food and to talk to a colleague. As the 'initiation' sheet (2.10b) shows, Hazel waves her arms, smiles and turns in order to try to get eye contact with Joyce. Joyce notices the movement and turns back to Hazel and talks to her whilst cutting up the food.

The third sheet (2.10c) shows Hazel's strategies for maintaining the interaction. She is an active turn-taker filling her turns in the 'dialogue' with a lot of eye contact and smiling. She stops and restarts her arm movements seemingly looking at Joyce for any reaction. She maintains her orientation throughout.

Joyce now wants to feed Hazel but finds her attention on their interaction rather than the food so she stops responding, looks away then finally turns away (2.10d, termination of interaction). However,

Table 2.10a: Observational assessment of early interactions
J. Goldbart and J. Rigby 1989

Name of Child: *Hazel* Age: *8 years*

Completed by: *JG & JR* Date:

Important factors which may affect child's behaviour:

Interactor	*J – nursery nurse from own class*
Positioning	*Sitting in small 'Rifton' chair*
Mood	*Very positive*
Time of Day	*Lunch time*
Setting, eg, distractions, familiarity	*Classroom – familiar setting, noisy with quite a lot of distractions*
Sensory and perceptual impairments	*Nothing significant noted*
Motor impairments	*Not independently mobile*
Additional individual information	

OBSERVATION OF CHILD IN A NON-INTERACTIONAL SITUATION

Watches own rather repetitive hand movements
Very little engagement with objects
Tries hard to get eye contact with passers-by

Table 2.10b: Initiation

Initiator: Target child ✓ Adult__ Other child__

If target child initiates, record child behaviour with a tick or comment.

Child behaviour	
(Attempted) Looking	✓
Approaching	
Touching	
Vocalising	
Change in Activity Level	✓ *Increased arm movements*
Gesture	
Showing/Giving	
Facial Expression (incl. smiling)	*Smiling*
Others Please list	*Changes orientation to try to get eye contact*

Is initiation successful? YES ✓ or NO__

If YES, proceed to next sheet

Table 2.10c: Maintenance of interaction

	Level of Maintenance of Interaction		
Child Strategies	*i) Interaction is Adult-Directed*	*ii) Adult-Structured Child Anticipates Turn*	*iii) No Structured Framework, Child + Adult More Equal*
(Attempted) Looking			✓
Touching			
Vocalisation			
Change in Activity Level			Continues arm movements ✓ then stops and restarts*
Facial Expression			Smile
Orientation/ Localisation			✓
Imitation			
Gesture			
Showing/ Giving			
Others Please List			

MAINTENANCE AFTER SHIFTS IN FOCUS

Can follow shift in adult strategy or focus? YES __ NO __ or Not Occurred✓

Changes own strategy within an interaction sequence? YES ✓ or NO __

* Tentatively

Table 2.10d: Termination of interaction

Strategy Used	*Termination by Target Child*	*Termination by Adult or Other Child*
No Response		✓
Response Intensity Diminishes		
Looks Away/ Closes Eyes		✓
Turns Away/ Changes Orientation		✓
Moves Away		
More Extreme, Please List:		
Other, Please List:		

Was termination INTENTIONAL ✓ or by DEFAULT? Please underline.

Was child aware that interaction had terminated? YES ✓ or NO __

Does either Child or Adult attempt to repair interaction? YES ✓ or NO __
If YES, turn to next sheet.

LENGTH OF INTERACTION: *Not all interaction was recorded*

Table 2.10e: Repair strategy

1a) Adult Repairs without cue from child: ________________________
b) Adult Repairs or Restarts in Response to some Change in Child Behaviour: ____

2a) Child Attempts to repair when Adult has terminated: ___✓___
b) Child Attempts to repair when Child has terminated by Default or Lack of Response: ________________________

RELATION OF REPAIR STRATEGY USED TO MAINTENANCE STRATEGIES

Strategy Used	*Continuation*	*Repetition*	*Modification*	*Exaggeration*	*New*
(Attempted) Looking		✓		✓	
Touching					
Vocalising					✓
Changes in Activity Level		✓		✓	
Facial Expression		*Smile*			
Orientation/ Localisation		✓		✓	
Imitation					
Gesture					
Showing/Giving					
Other: Please List					

** After successful Repair, return to maintenance sheet and resume recording of strategies for maintaining interaction as appropriate. Record as R, or in a different colour.

Hazel does not want the interaction to end. Her strategies for repairing the breakdown are on the final sheet, 2.10e.

Hazel at first repeats the strategies she has been using to maintain the interaction. She gets no response from Joyce who is not looking at her and therefore does them in an exaggerated fashion. She still gets no response and vocalises loudly instead. Joyce is unwilling to ignore this strategy and the interaction restarts.

Asif's interaction strategies are rather more limited. However he was observed with a very familiar person (Amanda) who waited near him to see if he would respond in any way to her presence. This response would be treated as initiating an interaction. Details are recorded in Tables 2.11a-d.

The initiation recording sheet (2.11b) shows that Asif does use some strategies which can be seen as initiating an interaction; he stops rocking, turns very slightly towards Amanda and his eyes seem to widen. Amanda sits down next to him and talks to him putting her fingers in the palm of his hand.

The next sheet, (2.11c) shows that Asif does continue his involvement in the interaction though this is mainly by responding to things that Amanda does. He maintains contact with Amanda's hand, ceases rocking for much of the time she is talking and orients towards her as far as possible. When Amanda stops talking on one occasion Asif seems to increase his pressure on her fingers slightly.

After approximately three minutes Asif's responses reduce (sheet 2.11d) and he looks away. Amanda, judging him to be tired or over stimulated gets up and moves away. No repair strategies are used by either participant.

Tables 2.12a-e give details of an interaction between Anna and her class teacher. It was set up specifically to try out the assessment protocol. The initiator, therefore (sheet 2.12b) was the teacher.

The third sheet (2.12c) concerns the maintenance of the interaction. Both Anna's behaviours and their level are recorded. The level is a measure of the work the adult has to do in order to keep the interaction going (See footnote[2]). Anna is an active more or less equal partner in the interaction. She has a wide range of strategies: looking, touching,

---

2 In relation to the observational assessment of early interactions:

Stage 1: the interaction pattern is entirely in the hands of the adult. The child fills in pauses or co-acts with the adult.

Stage 2: the adult still has the major role, but the child shows some anticipation of their turn. They actively take their turn rather than just fill a pause.

Stage 3: the child and their interaction partner play a much more equal part. The adult does not direct the whole interaction and the balance of turns is more equal.

Table 2.11a: Observational assessment of early interactions
J. Goldbart and J. Rigby 1989

Name of Child: *Asif* Age: *16 Yrs*

Completed by: *JG*

Important factors which may affect child's behaviour:

Interactor	*Amanda* *Very familiar community worker – does seem to recognise and respond to her*
Positioning	*in moulded seat*
Mood	*neutral*
Time and Day	*early afternoon*
Setting, eg, distractions, familiarity	*very familiar room, low noise level, others present but all actively engaged*
Sensory and perceptual impairments	*very little useful vision – perhaps light/dark discrimination* *Hearing 'untested' but seems aware of and interested in sound*
Motor impairments	*very little voluntary movement apart from rocking, a little head movement and finger movement*
Additional individual information	*has many epileptic episodes; major and minor*

OBSERVATION OF CHILD IN A NON-INTERACTIONAL SITUATION

Small rocking movements of head and body
does not engage with objects
seems uninterested in/unaware of surroundings much of the time

Table 2.11b: Initiation

Initiator: Target child ✓ Adult ____ Other child ____
Adult is close by and awaiting an initiation

If target child initiates, record child behaviour with a tick or comment.

Child behaviour	
(Attempted) Looking	*eyes seem to widen, but ? looking ?*
Approaching	
Touching	
Vocalising	
Change in Activity Level	*stops rocking*
Gesture	
Showing/Giving	
Facial Expression (incl. smiling)	
Others, Please list	*turns head and upper body slightly in direction of adult*

Is initiation successful? . . . . *YES* ✓ or NO
If YES, proceed to next sheet

Table 2.11c: Maintenance of interaction

Child Strategies	*Level of Maintenance of Interaction* i) Interaction is Adult-Directed	ii) Adult-Structured Child Anticipates Turn	iii) No Structured Framework, Child & Adult More Equal
(Attempted) Looking			
Touching	*maintains contact when A touches him* ✓		
Vocalisation			
Change in Activity Level	*stops rocking for periods while A talks* ✓		
Facial Expression			
Orientation/ Localisation	✓	✓	
Imitation			
Gesture			
Showing/ Giving			
Others, Please List		✓ *gently squeezes A's fingers if put in palm of his hand*	

MAINTENANCE AFTER SHIFTS IN FOCUS

Can follow shift in adult strategy or focus? YES __ NO __ or Not Occurred ✓

Changes own strategy within an interaction sequence? YES __ or NO ✓

Table 2.11d: Termination of interaction

Strategy Used	*Termination by Target Child*	*Termination by Adult or Other Child*
No Response		
Response Intensity Diminishes	✓	
Looks Away/ Closes Eyes	✓	
Turns Away/ Changes Orientation	✓	
Moves Away		
More Extreme, Please List:		
Other, Please List:		

Was termination INTENTIONAL or by DEFAULT? Please circle. *Not sure, I think he became tired*

Was child aware that interaction had terminated? YES ✓ or NO __ *I think*

Does either Child or Adult attempt to repair interaction? YES __ or NO ✓
If YES, turn to next sheet.

LENGTH OF INTERACTION: *3 mins approx.*

vocalising, etc which can be responded to. She is also sufficiently flexible to respond to changes in the interaction and to introduce some variation herself.

In this example the teacher intentionally terminated the interaction at certain points (sheet 2.12d). Anna was clearly aware of this and on the first occasion attempts a repair. We have endeavoured to get a measure of the strength or likely success of the repair strategies and how they relate to maintenance strategies or signals. As you can see from sheet 2.12e, Anna makes some pretty determined attempts to restart the interaction. These attempts must be recognised and responded to if Anna is to make progress as a communicator.

To conclude, I started out by claiming that many pupils with PMLD were being excluded from possible progress in communication by an unnecessarily restrictive definition of communication. If students with PMLD are to become intentional communicators they need to be treated as communicators whilst still at preintentional stages.

In order to assist the implementation of this approach in the classroom, certain assessment and interaction strategies have been proposed. First, cognition plays an important role in early communication. The relevant early cognitive skills can be assessed using Uzgiris and Hunt's Ordinal Scales. The data obtained can be used to inform intervention. In particular, I have suggested that learning contingency awareness via microswitch control might be a valuable approach with multiply impaired students.

The use of the Affective Communication Assessment has been proposed as a means for teachers to identify the idiosyncratic patterns of responses which might be shown by pupils with PMLD. These responses can then be given feedback in the manner described in mothers with their normally developing babies as a component in the transition to intentional communication.

Finally, I have suggested an observational tool for teachers and others to sensitise themselves to the behaviours used by students to initiate, maintain, terminate and repair interactions; behaviours which need to be responded to if these students are really to be treated as communicators.

This provides us with a communication curriculum which can be, and is being (eg, Aherne and Thornber, 1990) implemented in some classrooms; a curriculum which is open and accessible to all pupils with PMLD.

Table 2.12a: Observational assessment of early interactions
J Goldbart and J Rigby 1989

Name of Child: *Anna* AGE: *12½ Yrs*

Completed by: *JG* Date: *April 1989*

Important factors which may affect child's behaviour:

Interactor	*MB – Class teacher*
Positioning	*in preferred chair*
Mood	*positive – it's been a good day*
Time and Day	*late morning*
Setting, eg, distractions, familiarity	*familiar, very quiet, few distractions*
Sensory and perceptual impairments	*Nystagmus – affects gaze and eye contact additional visual impairments*
Motor impairments	*not walking without support can bottom shuffle*
Additional individual information	

OBSERVATION OF CHILD IN A NON-INTERACTIONAL SITUATION

Some vocalising
Mouths available objects or own hands
Some self-induced vomiting

Table 2.12b: Initiation

Initiator: Target child __ Adult ✓ Other child __

If target child initiates, record child behaviour with a tick or comment.

Child behaviour	
(Attempted) Looking	
Approaching	
Touching	
Vocalising	
Change in Activity Level	
Gesture	
Showing/Giving	
Facial Expression (incl. smiling)	
Others Please list	

Is initiation successful? .... YES ✓ or NO __

If YES, proceed to next sheet

Table 2.12c: Maintenance of interaction

	Level of Maintenance of Interaction		
Child Strategies	*i) Interaction is Adult-Directed*	*ii) Adult-Structured Child Anticipates Turn*	*iii) No Structured Framework, Child & Adult More Equal*
(Attempted) Looking			✓
Touching			✓
Vocalisation			✓ *and increases*
Change in Activity Level			✓
Facial Expression			*smiling*
Orientation/ Localisation			*some*
Imitation			
Gesture			*reaching? clapping? prompting clapping*
Showing/ Giving			
Others, Please List			

MAINTENANCE AFTER SHIFTS IN FOCUS

Can follow shift in adult strategy or focus? YES ✓ NO __ or Not Occurred __
when adult becomes less physical

Changes own strategy within an interaction sequence? YES ✓ or NO __

Table 2.12d: Termination of interaction

Strategy Used	*Termination by Target Child*	*Termination by Adult or Other Child*
No Response		*(1) (2) (3)*
Response Intensity Diminishes		
Looks Away/ Closes Eyes		
Turns Away/ Changes Orientation		
Moves Away		
More Extreme, Please List:		
Other, Please List:		

Was termination INTENTIONAL ✓ or by DEFAULT? __ Please tick.

Was child aware that interaction had terminated? YES ✓ or NO __ *for (1), (2), (3)*

Does either Child or Adult attempt to repair interaction? YES ✓ or NO __ *(1) Child, (2) Adult*
If YES, turn to next sheet.

LENGTH OF INTERACTION: *3½ mins to second termination*

Table 2.12e: Repair strategy

1a) Adult Repairs without cue from child: ______________________
 b) Adult Repairs or Restarts in Response to some Change in Child Behaviour: *(2) – though rather a negative one*

2a) Child attempts to repair when Adult has terminated: *(1)*
 b) Child attempts to repair when Child has terminated by Default or Lack of Response: ______________________

RELATION OF REPAIR STRATEGY USED TO MAINTENANCE STRATEGIES

Strategy Used	*Continuation*	*Repetition*	*Modification*	*Exaggeration*	*New*
(Attempted) Looking		✓			
Touching				✓	
Vocalising					
Changes in Activity Level					
Facial Expression		✓		✓	
Orientation/ Localisation					
Imitation					
Gesture					*? now taking hand*
Showing/ Giving					
Other, Please List					

** After successful Repair, return to maintenance sheet and resume recording of strategies for maintaining interaction as appropriate. Record as R, or in a different colour.

CHAPTER THREE

Implementing the 1988 Act with Pupils with PMLDs

Jean Ware

Introduction

In the summers of 1992 and 1993 hundreds of teachers placed a 'W' against every aspect of each SAT (Standard Assessment Task) that their pupils attempted. Then, in accordance with the law they forwarded a reporting sheet to the children's parents which effectively told them nothing about their child's progress during the year. Of course most schools accompanied this sheet with records of one sort or another which gave real information about the child, and of course the lack of achievement in National Curriculum terms was present before Key Stage 1 Assessment became compulsory. But the reality of writing 'W' in box after box on the National Curriculum recording sheet has brought home the difficulty of implementing the National Curriculum and its associated assessment arrangements with pupils with SLDs. This problem is perhaps most acute for those pupils who are unlikely ever to reach Level 1 in any aspect of the National Curriculum as has been recognised by Sir Ron Dearing in his recent report (Dearing 1994). As a result of that report the assessment and recording of achievement by pupils with special educational needs is currently being reviewed; and by the time this is published there may well be appropriate guidance on assessing pupils with PMLDs within the National Curriculum.

The modifications to the National Curriculum to be implemented as a result of the Dearing Report are wide-ranging, and Dearing's concern to address particularly the needs of pupils who have special needs means that there should be considerable benefit to pupils with PMLDs from the proposed changes. The report also reaffirms that the National Curriculum, while essential for all pupils, is only part of the curriculum.

This chapter therefore looks at the issues raised by the introduction of the National Curriculum with its associated assessment procedures for the education of children with PMLDs within the context of the 1988 Education Reform Act as a whole, and attempts a tentative examination of possible developments in the light of the Dearing review.

We can identify four major issues:

- The impact of the Act as a whole and the National Curriculum in particular on the concept of the aims of education being the same for all children which has become so familiar in the ten years since Warnock.
- The extent to which the National Curriculum can be implemented for children with PMLDs.
- What might be described as the interaction between issues one and two.
- The controversial question of whether the general aims are best achieved for children with PMLDs by implementing the National Curriculum.

Most important of all is the question of whether the National Curriculum can be developed in a way which takes better account of the needs of pupils with PMLDs, particularly in the light of the Dearing review.

Before discussing these issues however, I want set the context by examining the development of thinking about pupils with Special Needs and the National Curriculum since its inception.

Background

As originally conceived and introduced, the National Curriculum was seen to include little consideration of the need for flexibility and relevance arising from the diversity of pupil attainments, abilities and needs (eg Fish, Mongan, Evans and Wedell, 1987; Norwich, 1990; Daniels and Ware, 1990; Bovair, 1991). As Lawson and Chitty (1988) and White (1990) demonstrate, the construction of the National Curriculum did not address the potential tension of designing a curriculum for all while taking account of the diversity of pupils. This placed teachers of all pupils with Special Needs (and not just those of pupils with PMLDs or even SLDs) in a difficult position. They were aware of the need for modification and flexibility but fervently hoped for integration and inclusion in a curriculum for all pupils. For teachers of pupils with SLDs and particularly for those of pupils with PMLDs this hope of inclusion has sometimes been displaced by the spectre of re-exclusion. Whether or not this fear has any real basis it has been a potent influence on the response of schools and teachers to the National Curriculum. Additionally, teachers of pupils with severe or profound learning difficulties have faced a potential and often an actual conflict between what had previously been regarded as good practice and the demands of the National Curriculum.

Unfortunately, the initial concerns about the National Curriculum expressed by SEN 'experts' focused on the appropriateness of the proposed curriculum or the fine detail of time allocations to particular subjects, rather than the more basic issue of the relationship between aims and content. In particular the omission of lifeskills/personal and social education, so recently recognised as an important part of the curriculum for many older secondary pupils, from the National Curriculum subjects was seen as critical. By contrast, the churches initially expressed disquiet about ERA and the National Curriculum precisely because it appeared that pupils with SENs were being ignored, and that the difficult balance between the needs of society and those of the individual was being tipped too much in favour of those of society (as perceived by those currently in power). Unfortunately most of those within the churches were quickly diverted to the issue of the status of RE. Additionally, the SEN lobby was spilt along philosophical lines as to whether to argue for exemption or inclusion; with those who wanted exemption stressing the right of pupils to have a curriculum which meets their individual needs, while those who favoured inclusion saw it as an equal opportunities issue. Hence the opportunity offered by the introduction of the National Curriculum to examine how universal aims might be operationalized was initially obscured by more immediate concerns. Since then there have been some attempts to tackle this more fundamental issue; notably by Norwich (1992). Norwich suggests that there is a need to distinguish between a National Curriculum framework of aims and goals and the school curriculum which embodies them. He argues that it is a mistake to see common entitlement in terms of entitlement to the detail of the National Curriculum, and that it should be seen rather as entitlement to a common curriculum framework.

Access for all

Initially, those who saw the problem in terms of equal opportunities suggested that in order to maximize access for all pupils, earlier levels than that currently described as Level 1 were required (eg Peter, 1989). However this approach was criticised by some as implying that some pupils were not yet participating in the National Curriculum, and they suggested that the terms 'working towards Level 1' or 'working within

Level 1' were preferable. These terms quickly became accepted as 'politically correct' and later publications, even those that clearly include a progression in attainments below Level 1 (eg Fagg, Aherne, Skelton and Thornber, 1990), adhere to them. Indeed, *Curriculum Guidance 9* (National Curriculum Council, 1992) on the National Curriculum for pupils with severe learning difficulties states that:

> pupils should be described as working within programmes of study relating to level 1 until they have achieved the statements of attainment at this level. They then move on to working within PoS relating to level 2. Planning and implementation of daily activities should refer to pupils as working within the key stage PoS relevant to their needs.

However, some authors suggested that the concept of 'working towards' is illusory when applied to pupils who are unlikely to achieve whatever it is they are said to be working towards (eg Emblem and Conti-Ramsden, 1990). These authors argue that the use of such terminology does not assist teachers in making appropriate curricula provision. This debate reflects the tension which teachers have experienced since the inception of the National Curriculum between making appropriate provision and seeing inclusion as vital for their pupils.

Dearing recognises that assessing a pupil as 'working towards level 1' year after year is problematic:

> At present, where a child of 7 fails to achieve level 1, but has made progress towards level 1, this would be reported as 'working towards level 1' or 'W'. Pupils with special educational needs who continue to be unable to achieve level 1 at 11 or 14 will still be assessed as 'W' at key stage after key stage. Such pupils may have made, in their own terms, significant progress, but there is no way of recognising this other than through the teacher's own daily assessment.
>
> I recommend that assessment and recording of achievement by pupils with special educational needs should be reviewed. The School Curriculum and Assessment Authority (SCAA) should investigate ways in which the small steps of progress that pupils with special educational needs make are assessed, recorded and reported positively.
>
> (Dearing 1994 p54)

If this recommendation is effectively implemented it may go a long way towards answering the concerns of authors such as Emblem and Conti-Ramsden.

When teachers of pupils with learning difficulties initially raised concerns about the applicability of the National Curriculum to their pupils the response of the (then) DES was to stress its flexibility. For example, Fordham, the then Assistant Secretary, Special Education Division, when speaking to the Annual Conference of the National

Council for Special Education, argued that teachers should 'push the *inherent* flexibility of the National Curriculum to its limits' (my emphasis). (Fordham, 1989). She clearly included within this flexibility the possibility of modification and disapplication for some pupils, perhaps particularly those with the most severe learning difficulties. Fordham argued that this flexibility could be found within early DES publications about the implementation of the National Curriculum. However, the lack of specific guidance for teachers in these publications was reflected in the fact that, in 1992, the DES found it necessary to respond to the concerns of teachers in special schools by clarifying the position with regard to the modification of assessment arrangements. (Holly, 1992; SLD Experience, 1992). These Government statements made it clear that, where appropriate for individual pupils, standard assessment tasks (SATs) alone could be disapplied under section 18 of the Education Reform Act 1988.

Despite these statements, the problems identified by Bartlett (1991), that disapplying any part of the National Curriculum is seen as carrying worrying messages about the more general entitlement of pupils, and that inappropriate SATs reflect an inappropriate curriculum, remained very real for many teachers in special schools. Teachers of pupils with PMLDs were divided on how to respond to SATs, with some refusing to subject their pupils to what they saw as a totally irrelevant experience, while others saw the SATS as part of the pupils' entitlement; yet others were concerned to demonstrate the need for assessments relevant to their pupils, and saw participation in the initial SATs as a way of making this point. However, with the modification of SATs into (mainly) paper and pencil tests this argument has been overtaken by events.

While clearly taking on board the need for assessments which enable all pupils, including those with PMLDs, to demonstrate what they are able to achieve (see above), the Dearing Review recommends that 'simple, national tests' in the core subjects should continue, and that the results from these tests should form part of the information provided by schools for accountability purposes. It is not yet clear if and how these will be made relevant to pupils with PMLDs. However, the recent draft circular (Welsh Office 1994) states that special schools should publish National Curriculum assessment results in their prospectus (Para 145). This recommendation seems to take little account of the inability of such tests to measure the progress of pupils with severe and profound learning diffulties as acknowledged by Dearing. It is to be hoped that the proposed survey of good practice[1] will provide alternatives which

---

[1] To be conducted by NFER over the next twelve months.

reflect the achievements of pupils with PMLDs and their teachers.

As Bartlett suggests, the early DES/DFE responses to the concerns of teachers of pupils with severe and profound learning difficulties underestimated the potency of the fear of re-exclusion and, more positively, teachers' strong commitment to equality of access for their pupils. Disapplication seemed to deny this equality, but implementation seemed likely to leave many pupils' most urgent needs unmet. The concerns of teachers of pupils with special needs about the over prescription of content within the National Curriculum were shared by mainstream teachers, who also found that there was insufficient time to cover the whole of what was mandatory, let alone have time to spare for other areas.

Teachers' concerns over the conflict between what had previously been seen as essential parts of the curriculum for pupils with PMLDs and the National Curriculum (eg NCC, 1993) have also been addressed by Dearing. The slimming down of the National Curriculum should ensure that time is available for teaching skills and offering therapies and experiences which are not easily seen in National Curriculum terms, and thus address (at least to some extent) the issue of inclusion versus appropriate provision.

Despite these very positive outcomes from the Dearing Review, the implementation of the National Curriculum still presents a particular challenge for those working with pupils with the most severe learning difficulties, a challenge that can be seen mainly (although not exclusively) in terms of the tensions between balance and breadth on the one hand, and differentiation and relevance on the other. However, it is worth remembering that the implementation of the National Curriculum also presents particular challenges to those working with pupils with other types of special needs. For example, in special schools for pupils with severe emotional and behaviour difficulties this challenge can be seen in terms of the relevance of a curriculum defined in terms of subject areas as a means of achieving general aims to do with maturity and emotional well-being. But although this is an important question it is secondary to that of whether these general aims are relevant to *all* children. The issue of whether the aims of education can genuinely be seen as universal is therefore a critical one in any discussion of the relevance of the National Curriculum to pupils with SENs.

Universal Aims?

The difficulty of resolving these tensions has meant that the introduction of the National Curriculum raises with new force the issue of universal aims for the education of all children. For the past ten years Warnock's words have tripped glibly off all our tongues whenever the question of aims has been raised, they have become incorporated in the curriculum documents and policy statements of many SLD schools, and in the 1988 Act they have finally become enshrined in legislation, albeit in a somewhat altered form.[1] Whether they have guided, or should guide our practice at anything other than the most general level is another question. Yet *From Policy to Practice* (DES, 1989) and *Curriculum Guidance Nine* (NCC, 1992) make it abundantly clear that a curriculum which meets 'these general criteria'[2] is an entitlement of all pupils and thus, of course, of those with PMLDs. The entitlement of such pupils to have the whole National Curriculum available to them has been reiterated by Dearing. Furthermore, the strength of teachers' feelings about the rights of their pupils to inclusion has now been recognised (NCC, 1993).

Can the National Curriculum be implemented for children with PMLDs?

Two studies carried out at the London Institute of Education found that, in practice, the National Curriculum was being implemented with pupils with PMLDs in only a limited way. Johns (1990) looking at a class of teenagers with PMLDs found that the work they were doing related directly to only *one* statement of attainment at Level 1 from the entire National Curriculum core, although they could be seen as 'working towards' some others. Students in this class spent less than 50 per cent of their time on activities which could be construed as related to the National Curriculum. Farouk (1990) examining the curriculum experienced by a range of pupils with SLDs found that while he had little problem relating the activities provided for more able pupils to the National Curriculum this was really not possible for a pupil with PMLDs. Of course, both these studies were carried out only shortly after the introduction of the National Curriculum, and much work has been done since on how individual needs can be addressed through the National Curriculum programmes of study (see below). However, it seems likely that these findings are, nonetheless, representative of the genuine difficulty which teachers of pupils with PMLDs have in implementing the National Curriculum.

---

1 See Ware (1989) for a discussion of the significance of these changes.

2 ie. para 1:2 a) promotes the spiritual, moral, cultural, mental and physical development of the pupils at the school and of society; and b) prepares such pupils for the opportunities, responsibilities and experiences of adult life.

A number of publications from a variety of sources suggest ways in which this difficulty might be overcome. While early work concentrated on statements of attainment, and the need to break these down into small steps to accommodate pupils with learning difficulties (eg Webster and Webster, 1990) more recently, programmes of study have been emphasised as the essence of the National Curriculum. Additionally, while earlier work often attempted to demonstrate that the National Curriculum was being covered by assigning activities to subject areas, a process criticized by Kingscote as contributing nothing to the education of the pupils concerned, and arguably devaluing rather than enhancing good practice, more recently the emphasis has shifted to an examination of how the programmes of study can be used to achieve goals arrived at from an examination of individual needs.

Of course, it is not surprising that teachers initially attempted to demonstrate that they were covering the National Curriculum by any means they could, when their over-riding concern was to ensure the inclusion of their pupils. However, the imaginative use of the programmes of study can both provide a wider range of teaching contexts for essential skills and offer pupils the opportunity to develop these skills in meaningful contexts.

For example, Rose suggests that the National Curriculum's emphasis on collaborative and co-operative learning can be implemented in heterogeneous groups which contain pupils with both severe and profound learning difficulties using what he describes as a 'jigsaw approach' (Rose, 1991; Sebba et al, 1993). In this approach a group activity is broken down to provide smaller interdependent tasks which can be achieved by sub-groups of children, who thus need to communicate and cooperate in order to achieve the overall objective. The tasks are defined according to individual needs and abilities and thus individual objectives can be identified and addressed through the group work. Rose gives an example of how a pupil with PMLDs can be incorporated in such a group. However, as Sebba et al acknowledge, this approach is more suitable for some areas of the curriculum than others.

At the planning level, the staff of Glyne Gap School (undated) attempt to combine National Curriculum coverage with work on basic skills by use of a two tier system, with the second tier consisting of topics at the junior age and modules at the senior level to achieve breadth and balance. The modular system offers senior pupils the opportunity to experience a wide range of content covering most of the Key Stage 1 programmes of study. However, the staff have felt the need to design some modules specifically for those pupils with PMLDs, which underlines the particular difficulty of implementing the National Curriculum with this group.

Curriculum Guidance Nine also suggests a number of ways in which the National Curriculum can be implemented with pupils with severe and profound and multiple learning difficulties; through subject 'led' activities, through other subjects, through cross-curricular themes and through incidental teaching. However, in the examples which relate specifically to pupils with PMLDs it sometimes seems as if the process involved is still, in part, one of examining the activities in which pupils are taking part in order to identify, for example, mathematical concepts within them.

Another possibility is to examine, not particular activities, but curriculum aims or goals in order to find similarities between them and the National Curriculum. As mentioned above, one of the arguments which is put forward for including pupils with PMLDs in the National Curriculum is that of *entitlement*. From this perspective, all pupils are entitled to access to the same curriculum, and the issue is one of how that access is to be provided. It seems to me that the problem of access to the curriculum for pupils with PMLDs is a qualitatively different problem from the same question addressed to many other groups of pupils with SENs. Indeed one of the major problems identified by teachers of this group is that access to many experiences which would be considered as essential to all human beings (for example communication with others) is extremely difficult. Some philosophers (eg Singer, 1985) have suggested that as a consequence of such gross impairments, those with profound learning difficulties lack some of the essential qualities of 'humanhood'. Although this issue cannot be dealt with in any detail here, it is nonetheless a crucial one, for it has profound implications for the treatment of people with profound learning difficulties in all areas of life. From a more positive perspective the existence of learning difficulties so extreme as to present a major obstacle to participation in some of the most basic experiences of life, ought rather to generate educational aims concerned with enabling them to participate in those experiences. An aim which we might express as: 'enabling the child to participate in those experiences which are uniquely human'.

Over several years I asked groups of experienced teachers undertaking the Advanced Diploma Course in Education and Psychology for Special Needs at the London University Institute of Education to identify broad areas of experience which they would regard as uniquely human. These areas are shown in Figure 3.1.

Other groups considering the same question might identify slightly different areas though I suspect that there would be a good deal of agreement. However, these will serve to illustrate the process of developing curriculum from this general aim.

Figure 3.1: Areas of experience identified as uniquely human

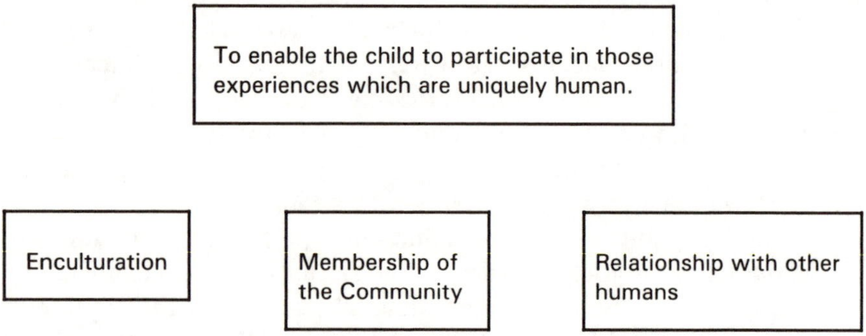

To enable the child to participate in those experiences which are uniquely human.
Enculturation
Membership of the Community
Relationship with other humans

Figure 3.2 shows the next part of the process – with each broad area of experience being further broken down and the links between them identified.

Figure 3.2: Broad areas of experience and links between them

To enable the child to participate in those experiences which are uniquely human
Enculturation
Membership of the Community
Relationship with other humans
National Community
Local Community
Relationship with peers
Own Cultural Community
School community
Special Relationships

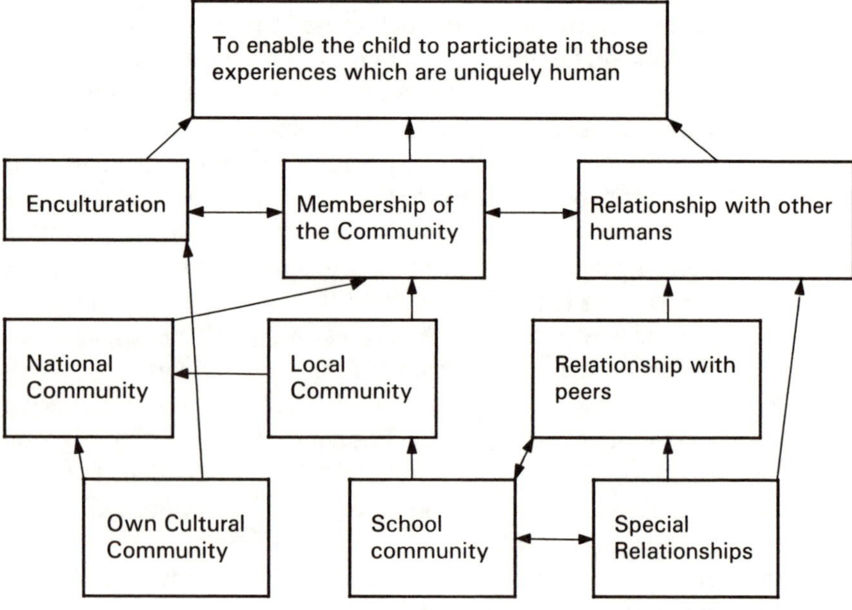

If then we examine one particular area in more detail for example, 'Relationship with other Humans', we can see that there are aspects of this aim which are immediately relevant to pupils with PMLDs (see Figure 3.3).

Figure 3.3: Relationship with other humans

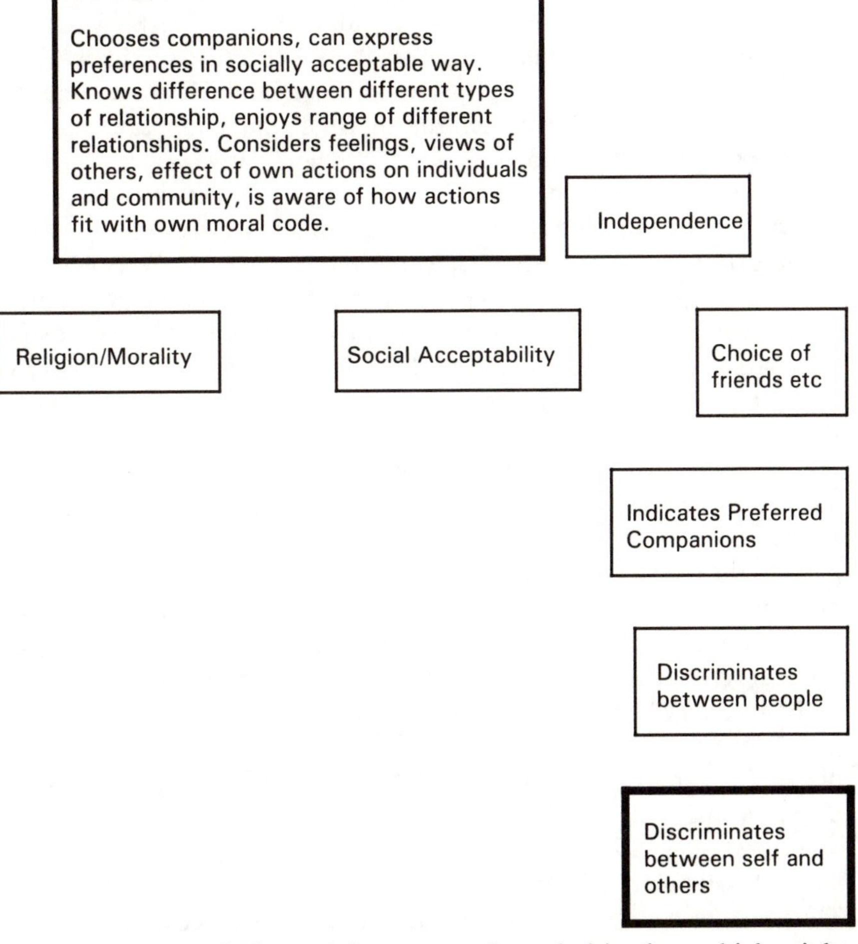

At the bottom of Figure 3.3 are a number of objectives which might actually form teaching goals for individual pupils with PMLDs, and (outlined with a thick black line) an entry point, which represents the earliest achievement which contributes to this area. It is possible to relate these teaching objectives to statements of attainment within the National Curriculum. For example, we might see a child who has multiple impairments learning to discriminate between their classmates by feeling hair as working on Science Attainment Target 1, Level 1: 'observe familiar materials and events in their immediate environment, at first hand, using their senses.' It would also be possible to devise teaching activities to achieve these goals; for example placing two pupils together on a mat in order to give them the opportunity to interact and highlighting their distinctive characteristics, eg long straight hair, could contribute to discrimination between people.

There are problems with this approach. First, it does not entirely overcome the problem of pupils being described as working towards goals they will very probably never reach. It is extremely unlikely that a pupil with PMLDs will reach the aim in Figure 3.3. This underlines the fact that the issue of whether the aims of education can really be regarded as the same for all children is not new. However, it is possible to argue that, in teaching the child to discriminate between people, we are contributing to their ability to express preferences, and thus to make some sort of choice between people, even if this merely affects who they are placed near in the classroom or who gives them their lunch. In other words, it is possible to conceptualise the general goal of relationships with other humans as being capable of being achieved at a variety of levels, only the most sophisticated of which is represented in the aim in Figure 3.3.

The second and more intractable problem is that whereas being able to discriminate between people is a worthwhile educational goal in itself, describing the activities designed to achieve this goal as science brings us back to the problem raised by Kingscote (1992): that it is difficult to see how this procedure contributes anything to the child's education. On the other hand, the child's experience of making discriminations could profitably be extended to include a range of familiar materials, and perhaps some which were not so familiar. Using the programme of study for science could facilitate both the individual objective of being able to discriminate between people and the experience of a wider range of different materials.

Interestingly, Sebba et al have recently argued that the personal and social development of pupils should be a central concern for *all* schools. Thus, at the most general level, the concept of universal aims can be supported even though those aims are not necessarily best achieved with all children through the same means.

Another suggestion, made by some authors (eg Ouvry, 1991) is that teachers of pupils with PMLDs (and indeed less severe learning difficulties eg Cornell and Carden, 1990) should pick and choose from the National Curriculum, selecting those parts which are relevant to their pupils at any given point in time. Thus each pupil would have an individually designed curriculum in which the National Curriculum played a smaller or larger part depending on individual need. This may well be the most appropriate solution in many instances, potentially meeting the criterion of a 'broad, balanced and relevant curriculum' but the curriculum balance would almost certainly need to be included in the statement for all pupils with PMLDs since, even with the greater flexibility introduced by the Dearing report, the National Curriculum is intended to take up 80 per cent of the available time.

In what sense then is it possible to implement the National Curriculum with pupils with PMLDs, and can this be carried out in a way which benefits the pupils?

According to the 1988 Act the National Curriculum is not intended to be an end in itself, but rather a means of achieving the aims set out in Section 1 of the Act. If the National Curriculum as it currently stands is not the best means of achieving these aims for pupils with PMLDs, it is also not the best means for many other pupils. However, as Norwich (1992) points out, we need to distinguish between the concept of an National Curriculum and the National Curriculum which is currently in force. Is it possible for the National Curriculum to be developed in a way which takes better account of the needs of all pupils, including those with PMLDs?

Options for Development

There are a number of potential ways in which the National Curriculum and its associated assessment arrangements could be developed, and it is to be hoped that such options will be seriously considered during the current review. This section examines some options for development and their potential for making the National Curriculum more inclusive.

Option 1 – A pre-National Curriculum curriculum?

One possibility which has been suggested is that there should be an alternative curriculum for those not yet operating at a notional 5-year old level – which would include all pupils with PMLDs, and no doubt a good many others. Pupils would transfer to the National Curriculum when they reached the appropriate level. This idea seems to me to hark back to Fordham's (and others) 1989 suggestion that the most appropriate course of action for some pupils could be disapplication. According to Fordham this would be particularly appropriate for those requiring a developmental curriculum, which is what those who suggest some form of access or pre-Year 1 curriculum most frequently have in mind.

A number of difficulties would be created by implementing this suggestion; first, and this is, I think, an overwhelming objection, it is unlikely that more than a tiny minority of pupils with PMLDs would ever progress to the National Curriculum. They would leave school having reached say, an eighteen month level, and would never have shared the same sort of experiences as their mainstream peers. There is little doubt that such a curriculum would be seen as very much second best. Second, there is an assumption in this idea that some sort of developmental curriculum – ie a curriculum in which the pupils are taught according to the normal developmental progression – would be an appropriate preparation for the National Curriculum. In fact there is little evidence to support this view. However, it is true that many SLD schools have been using curricula which are described as 'Developmental Curricula' for some years, and that there is a widespread view that this type of curriculum is appropriate for pupils with SLDs and PMLDs (eg NCC, 1993). Indeed this view was supported by the DES in a publication some years ago (DES, 1985). Nonetheless, there are some problems inherent in the use of a developmental curriculum with pupils with learning difficulties.

Such a curriculum embodies the idea that the development of all children is similar; progressing through the same stages in the same order, regardless of whether or not they have learning difficulties. Hence learning difficulties are seen as stemming from a delay in progress through the stages. This way of conceptualising learning difficulties has been so widely accepted that it now seems like common sense. However, not all experts in the field agree with the assumption that the best way to teach someone with difficulties in learning is necessarily to follow the normal developmental path. Indeed, as Kiernan points out, the view of learning difficulties as purely developmental delay is an over-simplification, which takes no account of the additional experience of the world that the person with learning difficulties has, and the fact that they may have experienced repeated failure during that time (Kiernan, 1985; Goldbart, this volume). Secondly, the level reached in the developmental progression at the point where schooling ceases may have little functional value. Any developmental curriculum potentially suffers from the problem that those pupils who learn most slowly never reach the goal. They may never reach the point where they are able to do what the designers of the curriculum consider to be the important things. Finally, purely developmental curricula are in some ways in conflict with the principle of normalisation.

Option 2 – Uncoupling assessment in Key Stages from chronological age

The second option is also in some ways linked to the idea of a developmental curriculum. This is the suggestion made by some people, that an appropriate solution to the 'Working Towards' problem is to uncouple the Key Stages from chronological age and assess pupils when they actually reach the end of a Key Stage. For example, following correspondence with the DFE, Wiltshire LEA in a letter to Heads of Special Schools, has suggested that:

> the progress and achievement of all pupils who are 7 and subject to statutory assessment should be reviewed during the first half of the Spring Term as part of the annual review...

and that where appropriate a pupil could then be given more time to complete the programme of study, their readiness for statutory assessment being reassessed the following Spring. (This process would presumably be repeated in several successive years if required.) The most recent circular on National Curriculum Assessment arrangements makes it clear that this is possible if in the pupil's statement a provision to that effect is included:

> Under the Act, pupils must be assessed at or near the end of Key Stages 1,2,3 and 4 (generally when pupils are aged 7,11,14 and 16 respectively.) It is, however, possible to provide for a pupil to be assessed at a later age by:
>
> a. **either**, teaching the child in a class where the majority of children are younger than he/she is;
>
> b. **or**, as provided for in Section 18 of the Act, by specifying in a statement of special educational needs that he/she will complete a Key Stage and so be assessed at a later age.
>
> Circular 12/92

The basis of this 'uncoupling' solution is the idea that the National Curriculum itself is essentially a Developmental Curriculum, and that in general children who are older are likely to achieve higher levels within it than those who are younger, not just because they have been taught more, but because they have developed and matured as individuals.

In some ways this solution is attractive: it means that pupils who are likely to achieve Level 1, but at a later age than 7 can be statutorily assessed when it is appropriate, rather than being faced with inevitable failure. Second, it legitimises what is in fact the case in many SLD schools, that pupils continue to work within Key Stage 1 (and indeed at Level 1) well after the age of 7. Third, it is a procedure which could be relevant not just to SLD schools but much more generally, and thus runs little risk of marginalising pupils with SLDs. Indeed, Dearing has gone some way towards this position with the inclusion of the Level 1 at all Key stages. However, few pupils with PMLDs are likely ever to achieve Level 1; consequently there is a real danger that this uncoupling procedure could result in the question of whether the pupil's progress is satisfactory being ignored. Most importantly (whatever the benefits of this procedure for some pupils) it does not address the crucial issue for pupils with PMLDs: which is that virtually all of them will be seen as working towards Level 1 for much or all of their school lives.

Option 3 – Modifying Statements of Attainment

Not surprisingly, many of those writing from a practitioner perspective have been concerned that there is insufficient flexibility in the National Curriculum to meet the needs of their pupils. Carden (1991), however, argues that National Curriculum subjects can be effectively implemented in a school serving pupils with moderate and severe learning difficulties with some adaptations to the statements of attainment. This option is related to the idea discussed above of implementing only selected parts of the National Curriculum. Unfortunately Carden does not describe the modifications made by his school although he does say that the form and content of the National Curriculum are still readily recognisable. Perhaps such modifications should be made on a national rather than a school by school basis. Aside from those attainment targets which, as the National Curriculum is used and evaluated, may need modification for all pupils, modifications of others might be placed alongside the main attainment target with guidelines as to when a pupil should be assessed on the alternative.

Possible advantages of this approach are the inclusion of the alternatives within the main body of the National Curriculum, and that the breadth of the curriculum would be maintained. Again this option is more relevant to pupils with less severe difficulties. It might work well for those pupils who were making significant progress, but for whom some aspects of the Statements of Attainment were currently unreachable, and for a few specific Statements of Attainment, such as the early science ones. It would not improve the situation for those pupils, perhaps the majority of those with PMLDs, who were not achieving any aspect of the Statements of Attainment.

Option 4 – Assessment on a broader range of activities at the same level

Another option, in some ways similar to that of modifying Statements of Attainment, is the suggestion is that there should be a broader range of activities at each level. Thus, there would be two alternative possibilities for progress, progress towards the next level and progress by extension of competence within a level. For example from MA3 Level 1 (which is concerned with additions and subtractions to 10) rather than moving on to Level 2 (which is aimed at the ability to recall the same number facts without calculating) the pupil could be given credit for being able to perform the same additions and subtractions presented in a variety of ways. One particular advantage of this method of proceeding is that it is potentially applicable even to pupils with more severe difficulties. (See below – more refined assessment arrangements). It is also applicable to a wide range of other pupils, particularly at more advanced levels. Additionally, consolidation of competence at one level would provide a good foundation for moving on to the next level. However, it has a distinct disadvantage in that it could lead to a heavier assessment load on teachers. Dearing's recommendation that the National Curriculum should be divided into core and optional sections could provide the basis for the development of this option.

Option 5 – More refined assessment arrangements

One of the biggest problems with the current National Curriculum arrangements (as recognised by Dearing) is that the present assessment instruments are very blunt ones indeed. It isn't really possible for a pupil to show any progress until they at least reach Level 1. This means that for most pupils with PMLDs no progress on the National Curriculum will be reported throughout their school career. The problem with any modifications to the assessment arrangements to provide a more accurate record of pupils' progress is that it is likely to add to the burden on teachers. One way of minimising this extra load would be for the teacher to help the pupil complete the task where they had been unable to do so alone and use a system of recording how much help had been given. Of course this would necessitate SATs which were not simply paper and pencil tests. This would have two important advantages: it would enable progress to be shown through a reduction in the level of help required by the pupil, and it is a form of assessment which is more generally useful for example for determining the likely amount of support required for the pupil to function in the community.

Additionally, work by Landesman-Dwyer has demonstrated that one way in which progress can be measured in people with the most profound difficulties is by an increase in the consistency with which they respond to a particular stimulus.

Conclusions

Although each of these options would potentially produce an improvement in the place of pupils with PMLDs (and indeed many other pupils) within the National Curriculum, none of them addresses the underlying problem of the conflict between inclusion and relevance or the fundamental issue of whether the National Curriculum – or at least part of it – is the most appropriate way to achieve the aims of education for pupils with PMLDs. Indeed, it might reasonably be objected that all the options for development make purely cosmetic changes to the National Curriculum. There is a real danger that the National Curriculum could replace previous good practice. Cornell and Carden argue that where the National Curriculum is not compatible with a special school-designed curriculum the latter should take precedence, since it has been derived directly from the needs of the pupils (Cornell and Carden, 1990). As these authors point out, the first question in the design of any curriculum for any group of pupils must be: 'what are we trying to achieve?' And then second 'how can we best achieve that with our pupils?'

The stated aims of the 1988 Act – 'the spiritual, moral, cultural, mental and physical development of the pupils at the school and of society;' 'and preparing 'such pupils for the opportunities, responsibilities and experiences of adult life' are very similar to the aims which many SLD schools have had at the beginning of their school brochures for several years. These aims were, in fact, derived from the Warnock report. It is clear from the sort of curricula these schools had in place before the 1988 Act that their staffs did not at that point believe that a subject-based curriculum such as the National Curriculum was the best way to achieve these aims with their pupils. It is partly the subject based nature of the National Curriculum which has created the tension with previous good practice.

Often, as I have already pointed out, before the introduction of the National Curriculum SLD schools had curricula which they described as developmental. In other cases they described their curricula as 'functional'. A functional curriculum is one which looks at what is required to cope (usually in adult life) and then sets about systematically teaching these things by what ever route proves most effective. In practice most schools had (and still have) curricula which were a combination of the developmental and the functional; with the overall goals being derived from functional considerations but the routes in general being developmental. Good practice in SLD schools before the 1988 Act, therefore, frequently concentrated heavily on the teaching of the personal and social skills which are necessary to cope effectively in our society. In some schools there was perhaps an over-emphasis on rather utilitarian skills such as survival cookery, but in others personal relationships and leisure skills were also included.

In some ways the National Curriculum itself could also be regarded as a functional curriculum with the aims being derived from what is seen as being necessary for society. There is, however, a difference in emphasis between the aims of SLD school curricula and the National Curriculum, with the National Curriculum concentrating on what society is thought to need from the individual rather than what the individual needs to cope with society. This emphasis on the needs of society is the second source of conflict with good practice in SLD schools where the needs of the individual are seen as paramount. It is important to realise that this is a general problem for all of special needs education and, indeed, all of education and not just for those concerned with pupils with PMLDs.

As suggested above, I believe that an appropriate way of expressing the aims of education for pupils with PMLDs is to enable them to participate in those experiences which are uniquely human. Although analysis of this aim will produce many goals which are functional, for example communicating needs, part of being a human being is being a member of a cultural group. It is at least arguable that when we have produced curricula that are purely functional we have ignored an essential part of being human, which is participation in a cultural community. If the introduction of the National Curriculum has had one positive effect for pupils with PMLDs it has been that it has reminded us that there is more to being a member of the human community than the acquisition of minimal independence skills. The National Curriculum has served as a useful reminder that knowing about science, history, geography etc can contribute to a full life.

Although the extent to which pupils with PMLDs can participate in these activities may, in some cases, be very limited indeed, there are several possibilities for combining National Curriculum activities with work on priority needs.

For example, Grove and Park (1994) in their curriculum resource *Odyssey Now* show how, through a series of Drama Games based around episodes from the Odyssey, pupils with profound learning difficulties can participate to some extent in what might be described as one aspect of our cultural heritage while working on important communication goals.

Those pupils who are hardest to include in the National Curriculum are probably those with the most profound difficulties, or having sensory impairments in addition to profound learning difficulties. Such pupils may need to be taught in a highly specialized environment in order to learn effectively. A possibility for these pupils is to be taught in that specialised environment for most of the time, receiving a specialised curriculum which is written into their statements as an appropriate alternative to the National Curriculum, while for a small percentage of the time they might join with another group in order to participate in experiences which were part of the National Curriculum and part of the broader curriculum to which it is important they have access. So they might, for example, be included on a trip to the science museum (with suitable provision for them to gain access to the artifacts on display), for this purpose.

Those with slightly less extreme difficulties could work on their priority goals alongside other pupils who are working much more directly on the National Curriculum.

For example, a teacher might be looking at the topic of 'food' with a class of pupils which includes one or two with PMLDs. For the group as a whole (or for some of the more able pupils within it), the teacher may have identified goals within the National Curriculum related (eg) to history and science:

> What sort of things did people eat in our parents' and grandparents' time?
> How was food stored when people didn't have fridges?
> How was it cooked?
> What did it cost?
> What causes food to decay?
> Etc.

These pupils might also be working on other individual priority goals for example in the area of handling money, survival cookery, shopping, etc.

At the same time, a pupil with multiple learning difficulties who was a member of the group might well be working on priority goals concerned with chewing, finger feeding or extending the range of tastes they had experienced and could discriminate. We might also be working on anticipation with another pupil through the smells of food being cooked. Or with someone at an even earlier level of cognitive development we might be working at identifying olfactory reinforcers, and using them to enable the pupil concerned to learn both to turn his head, and the beginnings of cause and effect.

I do not think that we could realistically claim that this last pupil was doing National Curriculum at this time. On the other hand, they would be working with their peer group rather than in isolation from it, and in a way which was appropriate to both their level of cognitive development and their chronological age. Most importantly, if our teaching was successful, we would be able to demonstrate that they had made progress, and in an area of real importance to them.

Similarly, a pupil who had challenging behaviour might well have priority needs in the area of (eg) learning how to be part of a group with other people without displaying aggressive behaviour towards them, or in the area of behaving safely in a public place. They might be included in an activity, which for most of the group was designed as a geography trip, with National Curriculum goals concerned with finding out about the local environment, and additional goals of being able to find their own way in the locality. For the pupil with whom we are concerned in this example however, the goal might be the much more modest one of walking on the pavement without having to be restrained.

None of these strategies will enable us to claim that the pupils are working within the National Curriculum in the same way as their peers without learning difficulties. They will, however, enable us to fulfil the broader aims in Section 1 of the 1988 Act by addressing the real issue of ensuring that pupils with PMLDs have a curriculum which is broad and balanced, gives them access to the range of experiences which other children have and still gives top priority to their particular and very special needs.

It would be easy to conclude from the possibilities for development of the National Curriculum which I have outlined that there is no satisfactory compromise between relevance and inclusion for pupils with PMLDs. Certainly, as it is presently constituted, the National Curriculum does not provide an appropriate vehicle for achieving the aims of education for pupils with PMLDs. However, this problem stems at least partly from the tendency of both government and educationalists to forget that the National Curriculum is not intended to be a end itself but a means to achieve the aims set out in Section 1 of the 1988 Act. If it is to do this for all pupils, including those with PMLDs, it needs to be made more flexible in the ways I have suggested.

The 1988 Education Act and the National Curriculum as part of it, therefore, has the potential to provide pupils with PMLDs and their peers with and without SENs with a curriculum which is both broad and relevant. However, this potential will only be realised if certain conditions are fulfilled. The National Curriculum needs to become much more flexible and to build on existing good practice. We, that is society as a whole, and educators and politicians in particular, need to face the issue of the conflict between the needs of society and those of the individual. Finally the National Curriculum as applied to all children, including those with PMLDs, needs to be properly resourced with materials and appropriately qualified teachers.

CHAPTER FOUR

'Proving integration Works' – how effective is the integration of students with PMLDs into the mainstream of an SLD school in increasing their opportunities for social interaction?

Richard O' Connell

Introduction

This chapter reports a study in which the experiences of two students with PMLDs in integrated and segregated settings were compared. The two students concerned attend a school which offers partial integration to students with PMLDs, based on individual need.

The integration of students with PMLDs into the mainstream of SLD schools appears to be becoming more common. In some SLD schools, organisational issues have certainly speeded the process of integration, although there may also be a measure of support for the policy within the staff group. If the number of students assessed as having PMLDs is too large for one or two classrooms, then some measure of integration becomes inevitable. One of the main arguments for integration has been a philosophical/sociological one – that our treatment of students reflects their status in society. This underpins the moves against the segregation of segments of the school population. However, the study reported in this chapter focuses more closely on educational benefits.

There has been limited evaluative research of the integration of students with PMLDs. Consequently, this study attempts to use evaluative methods taken from previous research into integration schemes for students with SLDs to examine an integration scheme for pupils with PMLDs. Several studies argue that increased opportunities for social interaction are an educational benefit resulting from integration. Increased opportunities for interaction with peers will develop social skills and provide a more interactive environment, where integrated students will be responded to and given more opportunities to respond. This study, using a very small sample size, suggests that the interaction of students with PMLDs with their SLD peers may be limited. However, there is research into the integration of students with a variety of SENs which suggests that interaction can be facilitated by preparation of students in both settings before integration begins and by schemes which are specifically designed to structure initial interactions. However, further studies are needed to see if this approach would have similar results with the integration of students with PMLDs into the mainstream of an SLD school.

Recent research

1. Students with PMLDs

Although there are many studies on the integration or 'mainstreaming' of students with disabilities, little has been written specifically on students with PMLDs, and there is almost no evaluative research. Ouvry suggests that students with PMLDs will benefit from the opportunity to develop and to generalize skills in a wider range of learning situations, which are more age appropriate. They will also be subject to higher expectations (1986). The proviso is added that a move to integration needs to take place gradually, with careful planning and adequate resources, especially staffing. Integration should not be implemented for its own sake, but where it is the best way to meet an individual's needs. She suggests that integration may not be suitable for all students and suggests as criteria for consideration that students:

> must show social awareness of their peers, some situational understanding and have acquired some effective learning strategies
>
> (ibid. p.159)

The article finishes with some positive, anecdotal evidence from a school where integration of students with PMLDs takes place, which includes reports of increased social integration and concentration skills, which are attributed to integration. Carpenter and Lewis have written widely about aspects of a structured integration scheme for students with SLDs. They also suggest that students with PMLDs should be able to participate in individual programmes, just as their peers with SLDs do, in the same classroom (Carpenter and Lewis, 1989). They suggest retaining the use of a 'special' classroom, for the teaching of mastery skills, such as visual discrimination, and integration for less academic activities such as horse-riding.

The Open University has produced several books which include positive accounts of cases or schemes of integration of students with a range of disabilities. One of the most recent includes an example of a school which has integrated its 'special care' (Corbett, 1992). An enthusiastic account is given of the school's move to integration, but little space is given to 'proving integration works'. The author clearly believes that integration is necessarily better than segregation, for all students, on philosophical/sociological grounds – there is no need to prove that it has educational benefit.

Soder argues that the view of disability as a 'social construct' can lead to physical integration being implemented, but that the disability can persist in an integrated setting. Such integration does not guarantee positive social contacts. He goes on to argue that integration can be used

> to deny persons with disabilities resources they want and need.
> (Soder, 1991).

Similarly, Evans and Ware suggest that students with PMLDs may be involved in a competition for resources in mainstream classrooms as numbers fall, especially if staff feel they are less able to benefit. They found no evidence that the integration of students with PMLDs aids curriculum delivery (1987, pp.159-160).

All the above use a mixture of philosophical and practical arguments, and all are British. Perhaps it is unusual to provide for students with PMLDs within SLD schools in America, which explains the lack of research. However, one Canadian study specifically evaluates the experience of integration of students with PMLDs. The study is based on the integration of these students into a mainstream school, rather than into the mainstream of an SLD school (Hill and Whiteley, 1986). The students were severely multiply handicapped, and had 'mild to severe mental retardation'. This illustrates one of the difficulties in comparing research findings – it is not always certain that similar populations are involved.

The report draws positive conclusions about the amount of interaction with non-handicapped peers. Unsurprisingly, it finds that the students with PMLDs had a higher interaction rate with staff and a lower rate with their non-handicapped peers, than the average for the mainstream group. However, it was generally the same small group of non-handicapped peers who interacted with the multi-handicapped students. This study supports the need for intervention to develop the interactions of both groups with each other. This is echoed by numerous reports of integration schemes involving students with SLDs based at Blythe School (eg. Carpenter et al 1986, 1988). These place repeated emphasis on the need for non-SLD students to be educated in disability awareness before such schemes begin so that positive social contacts will take place and so that they do not treat the students as helpless babies.

2. Students with SLDs

Although there is little evaluative research on the integration of students with PMLDs, some tentative conclusions can be drawn from research done on the educational benefits of integration with students with SLDs. One major study looks at students' achievement of individual educational objectives relative to their degree of integration, which was quantified according to measures of social interaction (Brinker and Thorpe, 1984). The effect of differences in functional level was statistically eliminated and the study was carried out with a large group (245 students). It concludes that interaction, specifically with non-handicapped peers, accounted for some of the students' progress in educational objectives. The scale of this research attempts to offer conclusive evidence for the educational benefits of integration, and suggests future research should compare the effectiveness of different models of integration in producing increased rates of social interaction.

This study certainly justifies the place of social interaction in research on integration. However, it would have been useful for such a study to have isolated other factors affecting progress, which resulted from an integrated setting, apart from social interaction, which was only responsible for 2.1 per cent of the variance in achievement of objectives. Also, no comparisons were made with the rate of progress of students in segregated settings, which may have been greater than that of the observed subjects. It may not be justified to expect such a positive effect for students with PMLDs integrated into the mainstream of an SLD school (Ouvry 1987, p. 51).

Other studies which focus on social interaction with students with SLDs produce varied results. Ware (1990) concludes from a study of two groups of six students in both integrated and segregated settings, that they *made* more initiations in a segregated setting but *received* more in an integrated setting. The author goes on to analyse the nature of the interactions, which show their non-handicapped peers taking on a peer-tutor role. This is supported by the observations of Lewis and Carpenter (1990) of the discourse of 6-7 year olds to their peers with SLD. They note that the discourse is characteristic of that towards much younger children. Ware suggests that students with SLDs are being educated for dependency in such a setting.

However, an earlier study of a much larger group of students finds that students with SLDs give as well as receive more bids in an integrated setting (Brinker 1985). Conti-Ramsden and Taylor (1990) support this, to some extent, in a study of teacher-pupil talk. The authors find that students SLDs *make* more initiations to teachers in an integrated setting, and *receive* more initiations from teachers in segregated settings (the exact opposite of Ware's findings with respect to pupils).

The Study

This investigation analysed the social interaction of two students with PMLDs in an SLD school. The two students concerned attend a school which offers partial integration to students with PMLDs. The students were observed in both an integrated and a segregated setting. Detailed assessments of the students were not carried out for this investigation, but it may be useful to include a description of their characteristic behaviours.

Rahim

Rahim was 10 yrs. 5 mths. at the beginning of the investigation. His file describes him as having severe mental retardation and epilepsy. Although he uses a wheelchair, he can push himself along and can crawl on the floor unaided. He is interested in his peers and surroundings. He moves around constantly and reaches out to explore his environment. He laughs or smiles to indicate pleasure and can vocalize. His most distinguishable word is 'bye', which he often uses in greeting sessions. He can point at objects to indicate interest and is beginning to use symbol cards. He can finger feed and drink from a cup unaided. He is generally cheerful and responds positively to attention.

Fiona

Fiona was 9 yrs. 4 mths. at the beginning of the investigation. Her file indicates the following conditions: Aicardi's syndrome, spastic quadriplegia, kyphoscoliosis, cortical blindness and epilepsy. It was also suggested that she had a hearing impairment, although the PMLD coordinator was dubious both about this and about her degree of visual impairment. It is difficult to gauge her level of alertness, as she often sleeps with her eyes open. Familiar staff listen to her breathing pattern, but it was rarely possible to do this as a classroom observer. She had a limited behavioural repertoire to indicate her needs. She appeared to have limited voluntary movement. She seemed to start slightly, if picked up suddenly. She seemed to smile twice (over several hours of observation), on one occasion after a period of working with an adult who had known her for many years.

It was difficult to judge such a change in expression as she could not accompany it with other expressions of her mood.

Her most common movements were opening and closing her mouth and eyes. The staff inferred 'yes' from her blink, and often waited for this response when asking her a question. Her first reaction on tasting a drink was to screw up her face, although this seemed to be a reflex action, as she would go on to drink thirstily. She had a similar reaction to food. She occasionally moved her head or limbs very slightly. She sometimes vocalized quietly or coughed, although it was not clear that she used this to attract attention. Staff exhibited a very caring attitude towards Fiona, who appeared quite fragile. The amount of feedback she was capable of giving seemed to be limited.

The two students involved in the study therefore provide a contrast in terms of behaviours relevant to social interaction.

School organisation

All observations were carried out in the junior half of the school. This has a Base room where students with PMLDs from the two neighbouring classes spend part of the week, in segregated sessions run by the PMLD coordinator. Rahim and Fiona have both been involved in this arrangement for five terms. Rahim has been integrating into the same class throughout this period, and Fiona has been integrating into the current class for two terms. These sessions also involve members of support staff from the students' class groups. The head has a deliberate policy of ensuring these sessions have a higher staff ratio than integrated, class-based sessions with mixed ability groups. Both students were integrated for three out of ten morning or afternoon 'work' activities, during the week. Daily greeting sessions took place in both settings.

Observation procedure

The students were observed for a total of eight hours spread over a five week period. Each session included continuous observations of one student's social interaction, made by the same observer throughout. Sessions averaged 25 minutes in length. Fiona was observed for five sessions in an integrated setting and seven sessions in a segregated setting. Rahim was observed for four sessions in each setting. Field notes briefly recorded setting conditions, ie. staff: student ratio, the nature of an activity etc. Observations were not made during lunchtimes, breaks, assemblies or when the students were being fed or toiletted.

In comparing the students' interactions in a segregated and integrated setting, several factors were of interest. As there would always be a higher staff ratio in segregated sessions, it might be expected that students with PMLDs would receive a higher rate of initiations or bids from staff in these sessions. Also, if their environment were more responsive, they might make more initiations. However, in an integrated setting, a more interactive peer group might make more initiations and responses to them. How much success in gaining a response to their initiations would the students with PMLDs experience?

It was necessary to make judgements about the quality of adult initiations. Ware suggests that initiations should be contingency-sensitive, ie. allowing for a response. (See Ware this volume). However, in this study, bids were categorized according to whether they were positive, negative or functional. Continuous observations were made of these behaviours so as to be able to preserve the sequence of the interaction. It was thus possible to record the success rate of initiations in gaining a response or in leading to longer exchanges (ie. if a response was in turn responded to and so on).

Adult or peer initiations were defined as any verbal or physical approach made to the student. An initiation or bid was considered to have ended if there was a pause of several seconds or if it received a response. Bids were assumed to be positive unless they had a negative content (eg reprimanding, hitting) or delivery. A bid was judged to be purely functional if it had no communicative intent, eg. moving a wheelchair. Also, it was noted if such a bid was accompanied by talking, which was judged to be a bid of higher quality. Even if most functional bids did not allow for a response, it is presumably better to be warned before one's position is changed.

Some latitude was given to the initiations or responses of students with PMLDs. Fiona's voluntary movements were counted as bids or responses – including vocalizations, blinks, and arm, leg or mouth movements. Her drinking was also included as a response. These actions were not categorized according to their level of sophistication. However, only Rahim's purposeful actions towards objects or the environment were recorded as initiations, eg. smiles, reaching out, vocalizing, waving, turning to look etc. It did not seem meaningful to note every motor act, as he was capable of making more sophisticated bids.

Results and discussion

The results for the two students are first discussed separately. All results are converted to rate per minute, or percent duration.

1. Fiona

Fiona's overall results are shown in Table 4.1.

In both settings the number of bids from Fiona's peers was negligible. The overwhelming majority of her interaction was with adults. As can be seen from Table 4.1 (Row 1), overall, Fiona received about one bid every two minutes – with a slightly higher rate in a segregated setting. She responded to about one in five of the bids made to her in both settings (Row 2). Fiona made similar numbers of bids in both settings, about one every ten minutes (Row 3). Overall about 6 in every 10 were

Table 4.1: Fiona's social interactions

	Segregated setting	Integrated setting	Overall
Bid received by Fiona (rate per min.)	0.56	0.46	0.52
% of received bids leading to a response	16.8	18.8	17.5
Bids made by Fiona (rate per min.)	0.07	0.08	0.07
% of Fiona's bids leading to a response	45.5	75	57.9
Functional bids as percentage of total	14.7	39.6	23.1
Non-verbal bids as percentage of functional	50	36.8	42.4

responded to (Row 4), with a higher response rate in an integrated setting. However, the numbers of her bids were so small as to make comparison across settings unreliable.

A higher proportion of bids received was functional in the integrated setting (approximately 40 per cent as opposed to 15 per cent) (Row 5). However, it should be noted that some of these sessions took place at drinks times. Offering Fiona food or drink in this context was counted as a functional bid. A slightly larger proportion of these bids were accompanied by speech, when in an integrated setting (Row 6).

Some interesting comparisons arise from examination of particular sessions. Four greeting sessions were observed. The rate of bids made to Fiona was higher in these sessions than at other times in both settings, giving an overall rate of 3 bids every 4 minutes. This suggests that these sessions may be more likely to lead to opportunities for social interaction, perhaps because of having a more social focus. Out of the 7 bids made by students, 6 were in greeting/drinks sessions – 5 were made by Rahim, reaching out to her in one session. One was made in an integrated setting, when one of the students reminded the teacher that Fiona had not had a drink. The other occasion was accidental – when a student used her chair to pull himself up. There was also one structured interaction between Fiona and a student in a segregated dance session.

One session was particularly successful – she made 5 bids (a significant proportion out of an overall total of 19), all of which were responded to. This observation was made partway through an integrated work session. Fiona had been alone for most of the previous 30 minutes (due to staff shortages). She then had a 1:1 session of sand and water play with a member of support staff, who was very familiar and confident with Fiona, and who seemed particularly skilled both in responding to and eliciting responses. She inferred communicative intent from Fiona's vocalizations and made contingency-sensitive initiations (Ware, Chapter 7). Session 6 also has a high number of bids from Fiona and adult responses, when Fiona was on a floor-mat, which made noises when she moved, acting as a sort of amplifier for her initiations. It gave immediate and contingent responses to the sort of initiations that Fiona is capable of producing.

2. Rahim

Table 4.2, for Rahim, follows a similar pattern to Fiona's. As with Fiona, the number of bids or responses from peers was negligible in either setting. Although Rahim can be seen to be at a higher developmental level than Fiona, there is no evidence to suggest that he

Table 4.2: Rahim's social interactions

	Segregated setting	Integrated setting	Overall
Bids-received by Rahim (rate per min.)	0.55	0.4	0.49
% of received bids leading to a response	50	24.1	41.8
Bids made by Rahim (rate per min.)	0.35	0.23	0.31
% of Rahim's bids leading to a response (pos. & neg.)	60	64.7	61.4
% of Rahim's bids leading to a negative response	15	29.4	19.3
Functional bids as percentage of total	27.4	37.9	30.8
Non-verbal bids as percentage of functional	35.3	72.7	50

received any more bids, despite being more responsive. In fact, his greater freedom to interact with his environment actually led to his receiving some negative responses – generally to his reaching for an object he was not supposed to have, or to his reaching out too roughly to a person.

He received bids at a similar rate to Fiona, about one every two minutes, with a higher rate in segregated sessions. Overall, he was about twice as responsive to bids as Fiona. His response rate in an integrated setting was 1 in every 4 bids, whilst in a segregated setting it was 1 in every 2 bids. So he was twice as likely to respond to a bid received in a segregated setting. His bid rate was considerable higher, than Fiona's – one every 3 minutes in a segregated setting, one every 4 minutes in an integrated setting. About 60 per cent of his bids were successful in gaining a response, as with Fiona. However 1 in 3 of the responses he received were negative. His bids were twice as likely to receive a negative response in an integrated as in a segregated setting (in total, 5 out of 11 responses as opposed to 6 out of 24).

As with Fiona, a higher proportion of bids made to Rahim in an integrated setting were functional. Unlike Fiona, only 3 out of 10 functional bids received in an integrated setting were accompanied by speech. No sessions stand out as being extremely successful. Although bids to and from Rahim are slightly higher in the greeting sessions, there is less evidence than with Fiona that these sessions provide more opportunities for interaction.

Only one peer bid to Rahim was recorded, which was part of a structured interaction in an integrated greeting session, involving being passed and then passing on a hat. Only two of his bids gained a response from his peers – both in an integrated greeting/drinks session. He received a negative response when he touched a student's leg. He also began a brief game of catch, with a cloth, in a fairly relaxed period at the end of drinks. This was the only spontaneous interchange observed between either of the students with PMLDs and their peers. Although this exchange was rare, it was difficult to imagine its taking place in the segregated setting. The only similar interchange was noted between different students, in the corridor, when the class was going to lunch. It is possible that more of these unstructured interchanges may have been noted if observations had continued into break periods. Haring and Breen (1989) suggest that use needs to be made of times spent outside the classroom to facilitate interaction.

Conclusion

It is perhaps inevitable that an investigation such as this points towards the need for more research in order to evaluate the provision for students with PMLDs in both integrated and segregated settings. Although the study reported here has focused on social interaction, it is recognised that measuring this alone does not measure the success of an integration scheme.

An attempt was also made to examine other relevant areas, but over the number of sessions observed was insufficient for any firm conclusions to be drawn. These other areas included Fiona's behavioural rate, on the assumption that a basic aim for her would be to encourage a higher rate of activity. Similarly with Rahim, who is capable of more sophisticated behaviour, his rate of production of intentional and communicative acts was observed. Both students' levels of engagement were also observed.

It might also have been useful to have examined other areas, such as the appropriateness of curriculum offered in both integrated and segregated settings. How successful was it in meeting the need of students with PMLDs? Another related area, which was not covered in this study, was the nature of the tasks given to students with PMLDs in integrated settings. Part of the time, there is no doubt that an alternative curriculum was being offered, and, in such cases, perhaps questions should be raised as to the status of the learning that was going on. It would be useful for future studies to examine how much of the time students with PMLDs in mainstream classes of an SLD school are being supported to participate actively in a differentiated curriculum, and how much of the time individual educational objectives are worked on as an alternative to the curriculum being offered to the mainstream students.

It is possible to compare this study to recent research with students with PMLDs, carried out in a segregated setting. These comparisons reflect well on the school. If all Rahim's exchanges with adults and peers (in both settings) are totalled, this shows that he was involved in a successful interaction every 2.5 minutes, overall, with higher and lower rates in segregated and integrated settings respectively. Fiona was involved in an interaction every 7.5 minutes. This compares positively with a study of four different classes, where average rates of interaction were about one in every 12-15 minutes (Ware 1990b).

Adults certainly made more initiations than the two students. However, in Ware's study, a response rate of 55 per cent to bids from students with PMLDs was only achieved in the most favourable setting, when room management was being used. Overall, about 60 per cent of Rahim and Fiona's bids received a response (though Rahim's included some negative responses). However, in Ware's study all behaviours shown by the students with PMLDs were counted as initiations. Ware and Evans (1988) also found that the more handicapped students are less likely to receive initiations which allow for response. However, though Fiona was more handicapped than Rahim, she did not receive a higher level of functional bids (which generally did not require a response).

The evidence from this study shows few major differences between the settings in terms of the type of interactions which students with PMLDs experienced. As bids from peers were negligible, and segregated sessions maintained a higher staff ratio, it is not surprising that both students received bids at a higher rate in this setting.

Both students received higher levels of functional bids in an integrated setting, but this could be accounted for by the observations often taking place at drinks times. These are the only differences between the settings which are consistent for both students. However, it is worth noting that Rahim was less responsive, and received a higher level of negative responses in an integrated setting.

The most striking aspect of this investigation, however, was the near total absence of bids or responses made by peers to students with PMLDs in either setting. The more able students encountered in an integrated setting were not providing increased opportunities for social interaction, one of the chief educational benefits advanced for integration. One possible reason is that the two students observed in this study spent more time than any of others of those with PMLDs in the Base room, away from their more interactive peers. The studies of social interaction noted above generally showed equal or greater amounts of interaction in integrated settings. It would be of interest to return to the school to observe all the students, and compare the opportunities for social interaction of the other students with PMLDs with those of their more interactive peers, in an integrated setting (similar to Hill and Whiteley, 1986). Other students with PMLDs may be experiencing higher levels of interaction. Staff might be skilled in the equal distribution of attention, even if students with PMLDs give limited feedback, but their peers may be less skilled.

One example was observed of a friendly, spontaneous interaction with one of the peers with SLD's – Rahim's playing of catch with the cloth in the drinks session. Another rare example of peer-peer interaction was of the structured kind – the passing of a hat between students to indicate whose turn it was to say 'good morning'. Initially, the first example may seem more attractive, simply because of its spontaneity. However, the second instance may be an example of a learning activity that needs to be repeated before a more natural exchange can become more frequent. Certainly, as noted above, research has indicated that, with the integration of students with SLD's into the mainstream, both these students and their non-handicapped peers benefit from preparation and careful structuring of activities to promote fuller integration.

This is supported by several American studies which have examined the effects of structured interactions on the quality of integration. Some of these studies advocate training non-handicapped students to act as tutors for younger handicapped partners (Kohl et al, 1984). The 'Special Friends Programme' (Voeltz, 1982) offers a different model of interaction: a half-way house, between cross-age and same-age friendship, is developed through structured activities during breaks and social periods. Such studies may have a vested interest in supporting the schemes they describe. These two systems have been compared using a combination of behavioural observations and ratings by those involved (Cole, Vandercook and Rynders). The study concluded that the 'Special Friends' scheme produced closer to normal peer relations, and might be more likely to last, while the 'Peer tutor' scheme produced teacher-student relations, which the non-handicapped students found were less fun!

A further study gives details of a successful implementation of the 'Special Friends' programme between mainstream students and students with PMLDs. Mainstream students received an intensive period of verbal instruction, combined with modelling of appropriate play behaviour, then teacher interventions were reduced, to allow social relations to develop more naturally (Cole, 1986). In this country, the integration schemes for students with SLDs based around Blythe School have been mentioned, with their emphasis on the preparation of students and the need to structure interactions. Recently, Lewis attempted to characterize those non-handicapped students (aged 6-7 yrs.) who were able to relate to their peers with SLDs in a less dominant and more 'enabling' way, so as to develop means of fostering this behaviour (1991).

Integration within a school may come about more gradually and without the same amount of apprehension that accompanies integration between schools. It may have evolved for reasons of organisation, rather than as a conscious result of planning of the sort described above. However, it still requires evaluation to ensure that students' individual needs are being met. It will be interesting to see the results of future research into ways of facilitating the integration of students with PMLDs into the mainstream of an SLD school, if it continues to become more common. Perhaps schemes such as those mentioned above can be adapted to encourage interaction between students with PMLDs and their peers with SLDs. Otherwise, this investigation suggests it may develop slowly.

CHAPTER FIVE

Microcomputers: Do They Have a Part to Play in the Education of Children With PMLDs?

Sheila M. Glenn and Yvonne O'Brien

In deciding whether microcomputers do have a part to play in the education of children with profound and multiple learning disabilities (PMLD), it is important to consider not only different uses, but also the theories which guide them. Many previous researchers have noted the different uses of micro-electronic aids and microcomputer technology with children with special needs (eg Hogg and Sebba, 1986; Warren et al, 1986; Behrmann and Lahm, 1984).

These would include their use as:

a) Record collection devices, laying out details of children's programmes and allowing for regular updating of their performance and progress. This would apply to all children as a general planning aid.
b) A communication aid with more able children with physical handicaps.
c) An electronic blackboard.
d) A reinforcer of basic skills using auditory and visual feedback.
e) A device to mediate between the child and the environment.

It is the latter function we wish to concentrate on in this chapter, as for children below a developmental level of approximately one to two years, some of the above uses are developmentally inappropriate. In particular we want to concentrate on an analysis of two major theoretical frameworks which guide such work viz. behaviourism and cognitive developmental theories, as these have distinctly different implications for how work should proceed.

The use of microcomputers to reinforce basic skills has been outlined by Watts (1991). He describes software and equipment, as well as arguing for appropriate use of technology.

It is not possible to review all the different types of applications: technology is developing very rapidly and in addition many innovatory applications are individual and unpublished. The reader is directed to Lovett (1985), Sandhu (1983) and Hegarty (1991) for general accounts. In addition the training of personnel is essential if microcomputers are to be used effectively and not just sit gathering dust (Yoshida, 1984).

Rather the focus of this chapter is on the theoretical perspectives which inform microcomputer based intervention in the early years of life.

Is the microcomputer useful?

Warren and Horn (1987) have recently argued that computer work with developmentally very young children is not appropriate as children in the first 12 months developmentally need interaction with their natural environments, and in particular with caring adults for development to proceed as normally as possible. It is true that in recent years the developmental literature (influenced for example by Vygotsky, 1978, Bruner, 1985) has emphasised the primary importance of social factors in development. This viewpoint holds that many of a child's abilities are first learned/developed in a social context via interaction with parents or more able peers, and can only later be used intentionally by the child alone. It seems indisputable that where children are showing social behaviour this should be a major focus for intervention programmes; indeed Nind and Hewett (1988) have recently argued that social interactions should be the central focus of the curriculum for children with PMLD. However, some children show few signs of social responsiveness, or are so physically impaired that they have little opportunity to interact with their environment; in such instances the use of microcomputer technology can be useful as a mediator between the child and his or her environment, as part of a wider intervention programme.

However it has been noted (eg Wallwork, 1986) that children with developmental ages of less than 12 months are relatively uninterested in flat, 2-dimensional visual stimuli presented on computer screens. He also confirmed Glenn and Cunningham's (1984) finding that where children with PMLD show preferences for auditory stimuli, they prefer to listen to nursery rhymes sung by the human voice rather than to simple tones.

Both the foregoing reinforce the notion that for developmentally very young children the main use of a microcomputer will be as a mediator between child and environment rather than as a direct teaching aid. In addition the computer can monitor the child's responding and hence guide the teacher as to the most appropriate level of development on which to focus.

A further issue raised in the literature in recent years is that of the educability of children with PMLD. For example, Dunst et al (1985) argue that microcomputer technology is important for showing that even very severely impaired children can learn and that such a demonstration can have positive effects on parents' and teachers' perceptions of children. Similarly in the UK since the 1971 Education Act there has been increasing interest in trying to create an appropriate educational environment for those children who show relatively little responsiveness to their environments, and whose developmental ages are likely to remain very low for the whole of their lives.

However as Odor (1988) and Aitken (1988) point out, computer technology is of little value unless used in a developmentally appropriate way, to complement teachers and improve learning opportunities.

Theories which guide the use of microcomputers

Perceptual competencies

In the last thirty years, knowledge about early infant competencies has increased exponentially. Innovatory methodologies have all indicated that infants are far more competent perceptually than had previously been assumed. From birth they can discriminate between stimuli, and recognise and prefer their mother's voice and smell. From a few months they discriminate colours, shapes, faces, depth and many important speech sounds (see Bremner, 1988, for an up to date review on early infant competencies). The techniques developed for investigation of infant abilities can similarly be used for studying the competencies of children with PMLD, and a review of such work is provided by Shepherd and Fagan (1981). Although they point to the paucity of work in this area they conclude that children with PMLD can discriminate visual stimuli, and moreover many can remember what they have seen. Similarly Glenn and Cunningham (1984) showed that children with PMLD in the first twelve months developmentally respond differentially to the same types of speech stimuli as do infants without disabilities.

Thus there is reason to think that children with PMLD may also be perceptually more competent than had been assumed. This viewpoint has been stressed by those educators who emphasise the importance of sensory stimulation in the early curriculum. For example, Longhorn (1988) provides detailed suggestions on activities and sensory curriculum planning based on her extensive experience.

However, some educators are increasingly questioning the exclusive use of essentially passive programmes. Behrmann and Lahm (1984): 'Do we teach children to be dependent?'; Brinker and Lewis (1982): 'handicapped infants may begin to lose interest in a world which they do not expect to control.' Dunst et al (1985): 'Typically educators have resorted to the provision of increased amounts of non-contingent sensory stimulation (e.g. bright colours, movement, music) in hopes that this will provide increased opportunities for learning and increase the likelihood that the student will attend to stimuli in the environment.' Many teachers would argue that it is possible to provide stimulation in a manner sensitive to children's interests (Glenn, 1988b, has collated practitioners' suggestions), but the questioning of this approach is prompted by a theoretical orientation which stresses the importance for development of action on the environment. This too has been studied in detail in the last thirty years in infants from birth onwards, and the emphasis has been on children's actions rather than their perceptions.

Theories of learning and development

Two main theories have dominated work in this century viz. Behaviourism and the Cognitive developmental theories of Piaget (eg see Piaget 1952). Both stress the importance of action on the environment and in particular contingency learning (where the infant learns that a particular movement will have a consistent effect and hence repeats the movement) but from rather different perspectives. The behaviourist is interested in the relationship between stimuli, the organism's response and reinforcement, without any interest in mental processes or representations which may mediate learning. Piaget, on the other hand, is a cognitive theorist who is interested in what behaviour tells us about underlying mental structures and understanding. From his point of view the appearance of contingent responding at around 3-4 months of age in the natural environment is a sign that the infant has moved from the stage of primary circular reactions (where the infant's actions are very limited and centred on its own bodily reactions eg thumb sucking and hand watching) to secondary circular reactions where the infant for the first time is beginning to act on the environment and monitor effects (eg infants kick their feet against strung rattles or hit out at toys hanging in the pram).

At first sight it may appear that the different interpretations are of only theoretical interest. However there are two major differences which have strong implications for practice:

(1) The first, and perhaps least controversial, difference relates to the inability of the behavioural model to specify development appropriateness when educational programmes are being developed. Thus Brinker (1984) argues that the selection of behaviour to modify or to teach has always been a problem from a behavioural perspective.

Furthermore he notes that as teachers have worked with younger and more handicapped children, so the problem of limited response repertoire has become more and more central. Within an operant framework intervention is based on the conditioning or shaping of freely emitted responses, but if very few spontaneous responses are seen then programme development is difficult. This is where a developmental theory to guide intervention becomes critical, and that provided by Piaget (1952) is still the most comprehensive and widely accepted, particularly when the child's action on his or her environment is under consideration. It is generally accepted nowadays that Piaget under-estimated infants' perceptual competencies, but his description of the child's action on the environment, and its development, is not controversial.

He argued that the general sequence of development is both universal and invariant, and subsequent work with children with PMLD has confirmed this view (eg Woodward, 1959; Kahn, 1976; Rogers, 1977; Macpherson and Butterworth, 1981). Woodward (1959) was one of the first to argue that much of the apparently aimless repetitive behaviour of young profoundly handicapped children could be seen as functional within a Piagetian framework. There are now available several assessment scales based on Piaget's theory, plus associated intervention programmes. See Hogg and Sebba (1986), Hogg and Raynes (1987), Glenn (1988a, 1988b).

In relation to multiply impaired children and microcomputer technology and microelectronic aids, the important point to note is that, within a Piagetian framework, particular behaviours are not important, but rather the levels of understanding which the behaviours indicate. Thus microelectronic aids which enable the child with minimal reponses to interact with the environment can be used to assess the child's level of understanding. Brinker and Lewis (1982) have provided an example of such a developmental hierarchy drawing on Piaget's theories for a child's growing understanding of ability to control the environment in the first year of life:

1. I can make things happen (but don't know how I did it) – Primary Circular Reaction.
2. I can make this reponse to make this event happen – Secondary Circular Reaction.
3. This response and other responses can make a variety of different things happen – Elaboration of Secondary Circular Reactions.
4. These responses are tools for finding out what will happen – Coordination of Secondary Circular Reactions and their application to new situations.
5. Different combinations of responses lead to different kinds of information – Means End.

Intervention based on this model is then based on contingency manipulation: arranging events so that they can be consistently controlled by infants. For example, Brinker and Lewis (1982) arranged a situation so that whenever an infant moved her arm a switch attached to a microcomputer was activated and the computer triggered music or toy movement. The computer could monitor arm and leg movements to see if the correct reponses was differentially produced (a step 2 rather than step 1 achievement). The computer also summarised information and presented it on a graph so that parents could see that their children were indeed learning.

Behaviourists are increasingly using such developmental frameworks to inform which behaviours need to be taught. So for example, Warren et al (1989) argue that one main use of microtechnology is to promote direct instruction of gross motor skills; various switches are designed to train for example head erect, hand grasp, using two hands together, and the onset of a battery operated toy is then triggered. Note the use of the operant model here: toy onset is being used as a reinforcement for the desired behaviour. In contrast the cognitive developmental model sees the child as acting on the environment, monitoring the consequences, and as a result developing expectancies about control of the environment. This is the more important of the differences between the cognitive and behavioural models.

(2) This second difference also relates to the different perspectives which guide educational practice for non-handicapped children and children with learning difficulties. Amongst others Cunningham and Glenn (1986) have noted that whereas the emphasis for young non-handicapped children has been on such things as spontaneous and self-directed learning within a cognitive developmental framework through

play and problem solving, children with learning disabilities have often been viewed as deficient in certain behaviours which have then been trained using behavioural methods.

A similar dichotomy can be seen in early contingency intervention work. Within an operant framework, interest centres on encouraging responses by providing contingent sensory reinforcement. Thus an ABA design is often used (baseline, experimental intervention, return to baseline) and effects on behaviour observed. In contrast, the cognitive developmental perspective emphasises the child's perception of the relationship between his or her response and events in the environment. In particular the detection of an expectation of causality and the effects on subsequent behaviour have been stressed. In this respect it is salutary to note that in recent years both animal learning theory (eg Dickinson, 1980) and infancy conditioning work (eg Elbers, 1987) have moved from a behavioural to a cognitive viewpoint: the existence of a central information processor is postulated, the function of which is to detect the causes of important events. In particular, animal research has demonstrated that mammals can detect not only positive relationships between response and reinforcement, but also negative relationships and lack of relationship ie that no behaviour that the animal can produce affects the occurrence of sensory events. This has almost always been demonstrated by looking at effects of contingency or non-contingency on subsequent learning, and has parallels in recent infant contingency work. For example, Piaget (1952), Watson (1966, 1972), Seligman (1975) have proposed that successful contingency responding in early infancy leads to contingency awareness and to a consequent increase in motivation to act on the environment. Both Watson and Seligman argue that when exposed to non-contingent stimulation infants learn the non-relationship and this will interfere with subsequent learning to produce those stimuli. So DeCasper and Carstens (1980) point out that:

> It is important to note that attention, positive affect and lack of fear arise because of the contingent nature of the stimulation; the inattention, neutral affect and depression arise from non-contingent stimulation; and that fear and negative affect arise because the nature of the contingency is, momentarily, uncertain or ambiguous.

Seligman (1975) has argued that if a child has learned that little that he or she does has any consequences, (which may indeed be the experience of many children with PMLD), then 'learned helplessness' and a lowering of motivation to act, may be the result.

Sensory stimulation, unresponsive to a child's state, may at the very best do nothing to help this secondary motivational handicap. Similarly the use of ABA operant designs, sometimes with the prior experience of non-contingent stimulation, may simply add to a child's uncertainties by violating any detection of cause that has occurred. Such a view accords well with many practitioners' unease with what they see as arbitrary (from the child's point of view) changing of reinforcement contingencies to fit with an operant research model. Even such advocates of contingency intervention as Brinker and Lewis (1982) and Dunst et al (1985) have used changes in contingency consequences to demonstrate behavioural control. For example Brinker and Lewis report that when a 4 month old child with Down's syndrome learned that arm movements produced music, whereas leg movements did not, then the contingency was changed to the opposite one. Dunst et al (1985) used an ABA design, plus non-contingent presentation of stimuli.

The infant literature has reported that non-contingency following contingency experience produces reduced motivation and negative affect, whereas prior experience of non-contingency produces adverse effects on subsequent learning (eg Watson and Ramey, 1972; Finkelstein and Ramey, 1977; DeCasper and Carstens, 1980; O'Brien and Glenn, 1989).

Unfortunately most of the experiences of the child with PMLD may be of the non-contingent type, due to sensory/motor impairments as well as developmental delay. There are also many studies indicating adverse effects of lack of contingent responsiveness on early social interactions and parental involvement (eg Blacher, 1984).

Implicit in contingency intervention strategies is the notion that control over environmental events is given to the child rather than the intervenor. Microcomputer based contingency interventions can then be beneficial for the following reasons:

(a) Children's smallest voluntary responses can be used to trigger stimuli.
(b) Accurate monitoring of responses is possible and change detected which might otherwise be difficult to spot.
(c) Sensitivity to decline in responding can be programmed as the contingent relationship becomes well established and eventually is less motivating for the child. Cause and effect relationships can then be made more complex to match and extend the child's development (eg see Glenn, 1986).
(d) A wide variety of environmental events can be triggered.
(e) Children can be occupied at times when individual teacher attention is not possible.
(f) Evidence of learning can be demonstrated to parents.

Research with developmentally young children with PMLD.

As far as contingency responding is concerned there are now many examples of successful learning in children with PMLD (eg Remington et al 1977; Haskett and Hollar, 1978; Brinker and Lewis, 1982; Glenn and Cunningham, 1984; Watson and Hayes, 1982; Dunst et al 1985; Lovett, 1985; Hanson and Hanline, 1986; Sandler and McLain, 1987) and some anecdotal reports of positive emotional responding and high motivation in such studies.

However, to our knowledge there have been no attempts to look systematically at emotional and motivational effects of changing contingencies. We have recently finished pilot work, some of which we report below. We only undertook this work after much heart-searching; we believed that we would see negative emotional and motivational effects and that these were undesirable. On the other hand we felt that such a demonstration was necessary.

Study 1

Pilot work was initially carried out with three children, one girl and two boys. One boy (R) had Down's Syndrome, a CA of 3 months, and an MA of 2.7 months (ie, he was very young and functioning at his actual age level). One boy (D) had Killian-Pallister's Syndrome, a CA of 4 years and an MA of 4 months. One girl (J) had spastic cerebral palsy, a CA of 12 months and an MA of 2.3 months. Children were assessed on either the Bayley Scales of Infant Development, or if they were visually impaired, on the Reynell-Zinkin (1979) Scales. These assessments are of course only very approximate.

Full details of the learning situation are given in O'Brien et al (1989). Different infant chairs were used to suit different size children. Auditory and visual stimuli were available and the children were judged able to respond to at least one of these. Approximately two feet in front of the chair was a vertical stand with a smiling face surrounded by four rotating arms. Directly underneath this was a loudspeaker which delivered nursery songs. The chair was placed in a unit which provided 8 infra-red beams in various positions; one of these was chosen to suit the size and ability of the child and when it was broken – for example by an arm or leg movement – the arms rotated and the nursery rhyme was sung for a fixed period of time. This was both monitored and controlled by a BBC microcomputer. In addition children were filmed on video cameras during sessions, so that any emotional responses –

smiling, crying, vocalising – could be reliably assessed.

Two of the children showed clear signs of contingency awareness, in so far as they increased their leg kicks over each session when they obtained visual and auditory effects. In addition they smiled during the sessions. The third child (D) showed no systematic increase in responding nor any smiling. He was older than the other children (4 years), and furthermore he had a high rate of self stimulatory behaviour (SSB) banging his head with his hand, grinding his teeth, and rubbing his legs together. We can only speculate as to whether these two factors are connected with his lack of contingent responding. Most of his ability to control events was by producing stimulation of his own body, and at the time we saw him he was inattentive to other environmental events. It is not possible to know if extensive contingency intervention at an earlier age would have prevented the development of SSB. However there is no question that these behaviours were grossly interfering with attempts to get him to respond to his environment. In contrast, neither of the two younger children were showing SSB.

Non-contingent sessions were given to one child (R). Here the computer presented the pattern of auditory and visual stimulation which had been produced by him in a contingent session. In the non-contingent session the child had no control over onset of stimulation. There was no smiling in the non-contingent condition and a large increase in crying (from 0.27/minute in the contingent session to 1.5/minute in the non-contingent session).

Study 2

The second study involved four more children (three boys and a girl) who were first given contingent sessions, then one non-contingent session, and finally a further contingent session. The children were a girl (A) with CHARGES syndrome, a CA of 19 months and a sensori-motor level of around 6 months; a boy (M) with Cornelia de Lange syndrome, a CA of 44 months and an MA of 12 months; a boy (K) with neonatal encephalopathy, a CA of 40 months and an MA of 2 months; a boy (N) with unknown aetiology, a CA of 28 months and an MA of 3 months.

Three of the children (A, M and K) showed increases in responding in initial contingent sessions, and also smiled in these sessions. In non-contingent sessions response rate decreased, and there were signs of negative affects (smiling decreased in all three), session time reduced markedly for A. None of these 3 children cried at all during sessions, although the fourth child (N) who showed no systematic change in responding, cried throughout and as a result spent relatively little time in the situation. Two children (A and K) had SSB (but not to the extent that it totally interfered with response to the environment) and this was used as an additional measure of effects of non-contingency. For both children the rate and severity of SSB increased in the non-contingent condition (in one case markedly). It would seem that as expectancy of control of environmental stimulation is violated, then so children turned to control of their own body stimulation. This may be regarded as another potentially adverse effect of the perception of the violation of expectancy of cause effect relationships.

In conclusion, we would argue that in the area of early learning, as in perception, there is evidence to suggest the same processes are occurring in infants with PMLD, as in infants without disabilities. Microtechnology has allowed researchers to demonstrate these competencies. The core of this methodology is the use of microcomputers as mediating devices, to allow environmental control and hence monitor responsiveness. This will help in the assessment of children's understanding, and may be useful in allowing children a 'sense of control'. However, children live in the real world, and it is important not to put too much stress on the artificial contingencies possible with computers. Children need to be involved in social contingencies and interactions if they are to develop as people. This is what comes first in normal development, and we must not lose sight of this in our enthusiasm to help.

Most of what we know about infant development suggests that infants are born with abilities particularly geared towards a social world, and we can only mimic a small part of this with microtechnology.

Microcomputers do have a part to play in the education of children with PMLD, they can improve learning opportunities but only if used in an appropriate way.

CHAPTER SIX

Classroom Organization

Jean Ware

Getting on for ten years ago now, a colleague and I conducted a piece of research into provision for pupils with PMLDs which involved me in visiting some 70 classes specifically providing for pupils with PMLDs (Evans and Ware 1987). On many occasions what I saw was pupils working individually. Members of staff would be occupied in teaching a particular skill to one child and the remainder of the pupils would be engaged with (or at least be provided with) a variety of pieces of equipment. Entering a similar class now, I much more frequently see the pupils in groups around members of staff who may be demonstrating an activity, or helping one pupil to participate while the others look on. Additionally, there are many fewer such classes. In 1984, when we conducted that survey, 59 of the 63 schools which completed our questionnaire had classes specifically for pupils with PMLDs. Now, many of those schools have integrated all or most of the pupils from those classes into the main part of the school. These changes have come about mainly as result of more general changes of emphasis in educational policy and philosophy. The National Curriculum has made SLD schools re-examine their concentration on individual work, and the idea that pupils should be educated with their peers wherever possible has gained wide acceptance, at least amongst policymakers.

There is a good deal of evidence that, whether pupils with PMLDs are integrated within other classes or catered for separately, the way in which the classroom is organised is important for effective provision. The purpose of this chapter is to examine the evidence for the impact of a number of aspects of classroom organisation on the curriculum received by pupils with PMLDs and to suggest ways in which classroom organisation can be made more effective in all classes where pupils with PMLDs are educated. However, as the changes outlined in the previous paragraph clearly demonstrate, classroom organisation is only a means to an end, and the first step in organising effectively is to be clear about our aims.

The nature and aims of education for pupils with PMLDs are discussed in detail elsewhere in this volume. The position taken in this chapter (as in Chapter 1) is that what education is about is enabling children to participate as fully as possible in the human enterprise and that a crucial aspect of this is concerned with becoming a communicator. However, although the aims of education may be the same for all, there is a wide diversity of individual need amongst those described as having PMLDs. The 1981 Education Act enshrined in law the concept that provision should be based on the needs of the individual pupil, rather than being category driven. Since pupils with PMLDs are a very diverse group, this principle is particularly important in deciding on appropriate provision for them, not only in more general terms, but in the detail of classroom organisation.

Classroom organisation can be seen as composed of three parts: organisation of time, organisation of people and organisation of the material environment; although of course, there are areas of overlap (see Figure 6.1). These areas are first dealt with in turn, and then overall organisational systems (which often involve changes to more than one aspect of organisation) are discussed.

Organisation of time

As I have suggested elsewhere (Ware 1990), whereas the determination of priorities within the curriculum and the organisation of time to reflect these are important for all pupils, they assume particular significance for those who learn most slowly. For pupils with PMLDs, therefore, decisions about priorities are crucial, but they are by no means simple; a range of interacting factors has to be taken into account in the organisation of time. Time has to be allocated between National Curriculum, non-National Curriculum areas and therapy, and between group and individual work, and decisions have to be made about what activities should take place at what time of day. Issues of consistency and variety in organisation also need to be considered (should the same activity take place at the same time every day or not?) and opportunities to be alone need to be balanced with opportunities to be with peers without adult intervention. Perhaps most difficult to resolve is the division of staff time amongst the pupils. An additional issue of major significance for teachers is the inevitable conflict between the needs of a particular individual and the needs of the class as a whole.

The principles on which time should be allocated to the National

Figure 6.1 Classroom organisation

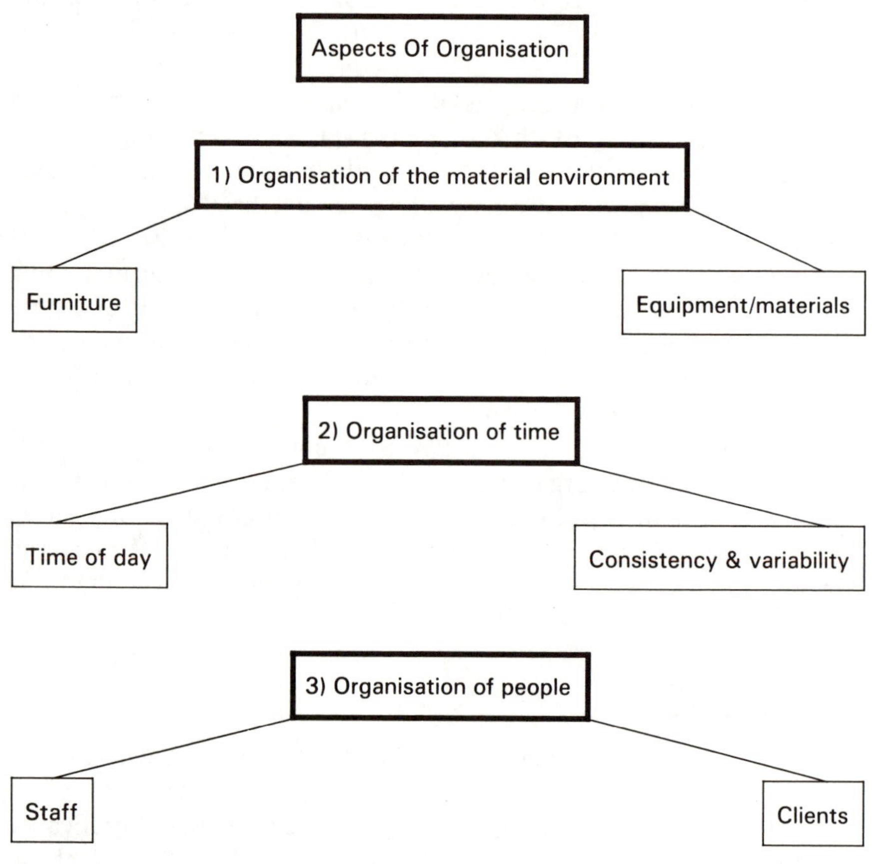

Curriculum has been discussed in Chapter 3, so this section concentrates on more general issues about the organisation of time.

There is comparatively little research which is exclusively about the organisation of time within the classroom. However, there are some relevant studies.

Time with peers

In the past it has often been assumed that pupils with PMLDs do not interact spontaneously with their peers, and therefore little attention has been paid to the need to provide time for such interaction within the classroom setting. Some research seems to confirm this view. For example Beveridge and Berry (1977) in their study of six classes in an

SLD school found that pupils in the 'Special Care' class made no initiations during the four hours that they observed. However, a number of more recent studies suggest that their findings may be a function of the rather narrow way they defined interaction. Ethnographic studies by Gleason suggest that prolonged social exchanges can take place between individuals with PMLDs (Gleason, 1990). In our research work (see Chapter 4 this volume and Ware, 1988, 1990) my colleagues and I found that a variety of interactions took place between the pupils with PMLDs we were observing, from vocalisation in response to another child vocalising to apparently deliberate touching. Such events were rare, but this could have been because there was little opportunity for them to occur. Perhaps of most significance is a study by Landesman-Dwyer and Sackett (1978). Working with individuals with very profound handicaps (their subjects were all non-ambulant and had an average developmental level of around 2 months) they found that when these children and young adults were placed upright and in contact with a peer they engaged in mutual touching and exploring behaviours despite the fact that in the normal ward situation they responded minimally to external stimulation. Furthermore, compared to a control group, those who experienced this opportunity showed more mature patterns of activity (they slept less during the day and were more active) even some time after the experiment finished. Allocation of time therefore needs to take account of the importance of interaction between pupils with PMLDs, although in practice, for these opportunities to be created, attention to other aspects of organisation is also necessary. For example pupils with PMLDs frequently need supportive equipment (chairs, standing frames etc) and use of this equipment can easily isolate pupils from each other. However, this problem can be overcome to some extent by positioning pupils who need to spend time in standing frames facing and within reach of each other, and time can be allocated to free play where two or more pupils are placed together on a mat.

Allocation of time to integrated sessions with more able peers can be supported on similar grounds. For example, O'Connell (this volume, Chapter 4) found that, although few interactions occurred in the integrated sessions he observed, on one occasion a game developed between a student with PMLDs and an SLD peer. However, other aspects of organisation also need attention if such sessions are to be worthwhile. (See below).

Division of staff time amongst pupils

Research shows that staff in a variety of provision for children and adults with severe and profound learning difficulties do not naturally divide their time equally between their clients/pupils. Oswin (1978), in her study of children with severe and profound learning difficulties living in long-stay hospitals suggests that those who get most staff attention are physically attractive and have learned a 'social smile'. Grant and Moores (1977), in their research into interactions between hospital staff and adult patients with severe learning difficulties, similarly found staff perceptions of patient attractiveness to be among factors which were associated with the amount of interaction experienced by patients. Other factors which appeared in Grant and Moores' study were the severity of the patient's handicap (more handicapped patients experienced less interaction) and their potential for aggressive or destructive outbursts (those who were liable to have such outbursts experienced less interaction). Similar findings occur in other studies (eg Pratt, Raynes and Bumstead, 1976; Paton and Stirling, 1974; Dailey et al, 1974). Most of these studies have been conducted in residential settings, but I also found an association between amount of interaction and severity of handicap in three out of four classes for pupils with PMLDs which I studied (Ware, 1987). A review by Kelly and May (1982) confirms that factors such as attractiveness are associated with the amount of interaction between staff and people with severe/profound learning difficulties across settings.

However, there is also research that suggests that division of staff time can be affected by organisational strategies. I found some evidence of this in my study. While severity of handicap was negatively associated with amount of interaction in three of the classes, there was no such association in the fourth class. In this class there was a form of Room Management running for most of the time (see below) and the teacher had a deliberate policy of spending more time with those pupils who were least able to occupy themselves (ie those who were most severely handicapped). In two of the other classes which ran Room Management for part of the day, staff time was more evenly divided between pupils when room management was in force. (Ware and Evans, 1989). Crisp and Sturmey (1984) also suggest that Room Management may have some impact on the uneven distribution of staff time amongst clients. In a much longer-term study of small residential units for adults with severe and profound learning difficulties, Felce and his colleagues have demonstrated that organisational strategies are capable of reversing the usual distribution of staff time amongst clients to provide those with greater levels of disability with more support (Felce, 1991; Felce et al, 1986; Saxby et al, 1988). The strategies they used included clearly defined staff roles and objectives; self-monitoring and organisation into small groups with one or two staff.

Scheduling of Activities Within the Day

There is little empirical support for the widely-held belief that activities which are more cognitively taxing should be scheduled for the morning. On the contrary there is evidence that some pupils with PMLDs (particularly those with the most extreme handicaps) may have cycles of activity which resemble those of a young infant, with alternating short periods of sleep and wakefulness (Landesman-Dywer and Sackett, 1978). For other pupils the effects of medication or the times of day when pain is likely to be at a minimum may need to be taken into account in scheduling activities. Alternatively, it may be beneficial to arrange for therapy sessions to be carried out at the beginning of the day to enable pupils to be as relaxed as possible for other activities. The clear implication of these considerations is that timetabling may need to be individualised.

Consistency and variety

Repeated occurrences of the same sequence of events, created by regular scheduling of the same activities at the same time, may help the development of anticipation, which is an important step in learning to communicate. It may also help the development of a sense of the passage of time. Additionally, one study found that children spend more time on task when consistency is maintained. A timetable in which there is little consistency from day to day is therefore unlikely to be the most appropriate for pupils with PMLDs. On the other hand, events which mark some days out as different from others are part of the normal fabric of everyday life. This suggests that a balance is required between events which happen at the same time on a daily basis and those which occur weekly or even less often.

Organisation of people

The people within the classroom can be seen as falling into three groups. The two main groups are staff and pupils; the third, volunteers, may not be present in all classrooms, and are certainly unlikely to be permanent in any, but they are an important group in many schools. Of course, the organisation of staff and pupils is inextricably linked; with staff:pupil ratios acting as a major constraint on the organisation of pupils.

The main questions to be addressed in deciding the most appropriate way to organise the pupils are: whether all the teaching is to be done in groups of various sizes or there is to be individual work for some of the time and whether groups are to be heterogeneous or homogeneous. A major issue in organising staff is whether they are to be responsible for pupils or activities. In many other areas the organisation of staff and pupils overlap; for example if some pupils are doing individual work, how will the remainder be organised? Who should work with which pupils?

Group or individual work?

Since the introduction of the National Curriculum, there has been a move away from individual work and towards group work in many SLD schools. A major aim of the emphasis on group work within the National Curriculum is to teach pupils to work collaboratively on problem-solving tasks. However, collaboration is, in developmental terms, quite a sophisticated skill. It is not usually shown by non-handicapped children before the age of about two, and few pupils with PMLDs are likely to be operating at this level. Not surprisingly, therefore, most group work in which pupils with PMLDs are involved is not of the type envisaged in the National Curriculum. Group work with pupils with PMLDs is much more likely to consist of each pupil in the group 'having a turn', with some instruction/demonstration to the whole group. Two important findings which emerge from research comparing groups of this type with individual work are that the comparative effectiveness of these two types of organisation depends on the severity of handicap of the individuals involved and the task being taught. In contrast with studies examining the teaching of academic skills to children with moderate or severe learning difficulties which have found that group instruction is equal or superior to individual teaching (eg Fink and Sandall, 1980; Storm and Willis, 1978; Alberto, 1980) Westling et al (1982) report that individual teaching was more effective than small groups for children with *profound* learning difficulties.

Sturmey and Crisp summarise the findings from this research in a list of conditions which are necessary for group teaching to be effective:

Conditions Necessary for Effective Group Teaching

1. Selecting students who do not disrupt the smooth running of the group.
2. Selecting students who can imitate to maximize modelling.
3. Including peer models.
4. Selecting goals that are shared by the group.

5. Choosing tasks that can be observed easily to facilitate modelling.
6. Choosing tasks which involve simple responses.
7. Suitable group size.

An examination of these conditions suggests that if group teaching is to be used the groups should be homogeneous – that is, they should consist of pupils at the same level needing to learn the same thing (eg Derbyshire Language groups). Indeed, research from other areas of education reviewed by Brophy and Good (Brophy, 1979; Good, 1979) suggests that in organisational terms teaching homogeneous groups makes the most effective use of staff time. In practice, however, it will rarely be possible to create a truly homogeneous group in a class of pupils with PMLDs, although in particular curriculum areas there may be two or more pupils operating at similar levels. Additionally, the emphasis on imitation in conditions 2, 3 and 5 suggests that group teaching may be inappropriate for those pupils with PMLDs who have not yet reached this stage. However, learning to solve problems collaboratively and efficient use of staff time are not the only benefits to be derived from group work; working in groups may increase a pupil's awareness of group identity and sense of belonging. In an integrated class, creating homogeneous groups will almost inevitably lead to pupils with PMLDs working separately from their SLD peers, thus losing an important benefit of group work for all the pupils. On the other hand, unless heterogeneous groups are carefully planned, teachers are likely to direct their efforts in an undifferentiated way.

Scripted groups

Is it possible to combine the benefits of group and individual teaching? One form of organisation which offers the possibility of working with heterogeneous groups without losing the benefits of individual work is to use scripted groups. These are a development of the inter-sequential groups described by Brown et al (1980). As described by Brown et al, an intersequential group is a group in which the answer or action required of each pupil is consequent on the answer or action of the preceding pupil in the group. In addition, Brown et al stress the importance of individual recording of such group teaching sessions. The problem with groups such as these is that the interactions between the pupils can seem rather contrived and that usually only two group members are involved at any one time.

In a scripted group, the interactions between the pupils are, as far as possible, naturalistic and meaningful. The teacher follows a script in order to enable each individual to work on goals that are a priority for them, and to ensure that progress is accurately recorded. Ideally the script will be flexible enough to facilitate development as the pupils progress.

The example which follows illustrates how scripted groups can be used in a variety of situations as a means of involving pupils with PMLDs meaningfully in heterogeneous groups.

Example : Preparing a meal of 'Something' on Toast

There are four students involved in this group who have been chosen to work together because of the likelihood that they will eventually go to the same group home.

Mary is a fairly able 15 year old who has good verbal and memory skills. She is also good at organising others but needs to learn to do so in a way that respects their autonomy. Mary can prepare a snack for herself and others but needs to widen her repertoire beyond canned foods.

Jamie is 16, he has fairly profound learning difficulties. Jamie has some communication skills, he is learning to eye point in order to choose, and vocalises loudly to attract attention. Jamie has a wheelchair, but does not operate this himself, he needs to be fed at mealtimes, and will turn his head away if he does not want a particular item. He has fairly strong preferences for different types of food, and particularly likes cheese. He needs to communicate his wishes to peers.

Paul is also 15, he is less able than Mary, he can make and butter toast for himself, he needs to learn to cooperate with others in preparing a meal. Paul is fond of Jamie and often spends part of his break time pushing Jamie around in his wheelchair. He needs to learn to treat Jamie as an equal rather than as a baby.

Chris is 16, she will attempt to prepare a snack for herself and others, making one piece of toast for each person, but needs to use appropriate quantities of other things such as beans.

The long term aim is that the students will be able to cooperate in preparing a snack without staff supervision. Individual aims are of two sorts, those that are directly related to this long term aim and those that relate to other priority needs for the students involved.

Mary: Assist others to choose what to have on their toast. Tell Chris how many people want each thing. Prepare cheese if required, and make toasted cheese.

Paul: Place toast in toaster for whole group, ask Jamie to watch toast and position him appropriately. Lay table. Remove toast from toaster when called by Jamie. Butter toast as required.

Jamie: To demonstrate that he knows that they are going to do cooking. To choose what he will have on his toast without help from a member of staff. To call Paul when toast is ready.

Chris: Decide on amounts of various foods required, according to number of people having each type. Heat canned foods in saucepan.

Over time, roles in the preparation of the snack would as far as possible be rotated, to enable the students to generalise their skills.

The Script:

At the start of the session, the teacher sits with the students and goes through the task to be performed. She begins by reminding the students that they should watch and listen all the time so they can help if someone else is having difficulty because it's everybody's responsibility to make sure the job is successfully completed.

Teacher: Jamie, what are we going to do now? (She shows Jamie three symbols for different school activities including cooking). If he eyepoints to one of the symbols the teacher asks: Paul, is he right? If Jamie does not eyepoint to the cooking symbol, the teacher involves the rest of the group.

Teacher: What are we going to do now? Jamie, can you show me which one says Cooking?

Chris, who's going to decide what to cook? When Chris has replied if she does not indicate that everyone will be able to choose, the teacher waits a few moments, and then if there is no spontaneous reaction from the remainder of the group asks: Is she right?

Teacher: So how are we going to find out what everyone wants, Mary?

... the conversation proceeds in this way until the whole process of preparing the snack has been covered and the part each student will play has been identified. Once actual preparation begins the teacher uses the script to prompt the students where necessary. For example if Paul remains with Jamie after placing him so that he can watch the toast, the teacher may ask: 'Who's watching the toast?', as a prompt to the others to ask Paul to leave Jamie to watch the toast and get on with laying the table.

For the more able students, as they become used to this way of working, it ensures that they listen and try and work out what to do or say next for themselves while someone else is the focus of the teacher's attention. For students with profound and multiple learning difficulties it enhances their prestige by giving them a real role in the group and by putting the emphasis on group responsibility for the successful completion of the task, in addition to ensuring that their individual needs are addressed within the group situation.

Jigsawing and other approaches

A somewhat similar approach, which he describes as 'jigsawing', is suggested by Rose as a way in which the National Curriculum emphasis on collaborative groups can be implemented with heterogeneous groups in an SLD school (see Chapter 3). Sebba et al (1993) also discuss a number of ways of promoting effective group work with heterogeneous groups of pupils with SLDs. Although they do not discuss the use of these approaches with pupils with PMLDs, their suggestion that the skill of working in a group needs to be introduced gradually, would be particularly applicable to heterogeneous groups containing pupils with both SLDs and PMLDs.

Organisation of staff

One way in which schools for pupils with SLDs differ from most other schools (including many special schools) is that there are invariably two or more adults in each classroom. In addition to the teacher (or, in some cases, teachers) there will be assistants, volunteers and other professionals, such as physiotherapists. Research in adult provision shows that where there are a number of staff working with a group of clients, careful organisation is necessary to ensure that staff are effectively employed. For example, Mansell et al (1982) found that increasing staff:client ratios did not result in increased staff-client interaction unless each member of staff was given specific duties.

A number of methods have been devised for dealing with this problem. These can be divided into schemes which make each staff member responsible for particular pupils, those that make each staff member responsible for particular activities, keyworker schemes, and those that give each member of staff a specific role.

Key worker schemes assign particular responsibility for each pupil to a particular member of staff. Advantages of these schemes include: Each member of staff getting to know a few pupils particularly well and being in a good position to understand the meaning of their attempts at communication and the key worker acting as an advocate for the pupils they are responsible for. However, keyworker schemes address only one aspect of staff organisation, and do not necessarily facilitate appropriate distribution of staff time between pupils.

Dividing roles between adults

In general, research has found that staff are deployed more effectively (eg clients/pupils spend more time on task) when they are assigned specific roles, (eg Hart and Risley, 1976). The most well known scheme assigning specific roles to individual members of staff is Room Management (Porterfield and Blunden, 1977), and the remainder of this chapter is concerned with the various versions of Room Management which have been tried in classes for pupils with severe and profound learning difficulties. However, Room Management is not the only way in which roles can be divided between staff, indeed it was developed out of a simpler form of organisation known as 'zoning' (Lelaurin and Risley, 1972). In zoning, each member of staff has responsibility for a particular activity and the pupils move to a new activity individually as they are ready.

Room Management

As originally designed, Room Management is not simply a method of giving each member of staff a clear role. It is based on two principles, that individual teaching sessions are the most effective way of ensuring that people with severe or profound learning difficulties acquire new skills (the research reviewed above supports this view in the case of people with profound learning difficulties, and also to some extent for people with severe learning difficulties) and that attention is a generalised reinforcer. The basic aim in Room Management is therefore to 'free-up' one member of staff to work individually with each client/pupil in turn. The remaining jobs which have to be done are divided between the remaining staff.

Room Management was developed originally for use with adults in the Special Needs Units of Adult Training Centres – and is therefore potentially very appropriate for use in classes where all the pupils have PMLDs, although it is worth noting that many people who attend Special Needs Units in ATCs would not be regarded a having PMLDs within the education system. In general they would be likely to be more intellectually able, more likely to have challenging behaviours, and less likely to have profound physical disabilities than pupils classified as having PMLDs.

In the setting where the original Room Management scheme was introduced there was one group of staff responsible for the physical needs of the clients (care assistants) and another group (instructors and supervisors) responsible for the clients' programme. It was this second group of staff who were involved in the Room Management scheme, while the care assistants continued to deal with toileting etc. There were three roles for staff in the original scheme, each with a clearly defined job description: Room Manager, Individual Worker, and Individual Helper.

The **Individual Worker** was responsible for conducting individual teaching programmes with each client in turn, in a room separate from the main activity room. The **Room Manager** was responsible for keeping those who were not being worked with individually engaged with holding activities. They were to provide each client with a choice of activities, pay attention to those who were engaged with materials and briefly prompt those who were not engaged. The **Individual Helper** was responsible for staying in the room with the Room Manager in order to deal with any emergencies, visitors etc, and spent the remainder of their time helping clients with the materials they were working with. In subsequent versions of Room Management, this role has usually also included responsibility for toileting (see below).

Duties of Room Manager

1. Tidy the room and make sure materials are convenient.
2. Tell the previous room manager that he/she is ready to take over.
3. Give each client a material or opportunity to be busy, eg game, song.
4. Place other materials within each client's reach if appropriate.
5. Make at least 12 contacts to *busy* clients (tally each contact).
6. Comment approvingly about the clients' activities.
7. *Briefly* prompt clients who do not begin using materials or participating in activity.
8. Offer a choice of alternative materials or activity when clients complete a task.
9. Stay in the room unless specifically relieved by another member of staff.

(Porterfield and Blunden 1977)

However, Room Management includes other important components besides clearly defined roles. Staff were trained up to a specified criterion in each of the roles, and after training, their performance was periodically monitored by line managers. Additionally, the organisation of furniture for the Room Management Period was specified – clients *sat* at *tables* arranged in horseshoe shape to enable the room manager to contact them easily and additional holding activities were supplied to promote high engagement.

In this original study, Room Management was compared with a baseline condition and with the introduction of new materials alone. During Room Management, direct engagement increased to around 80 per cent (from a baseline figure of 31 per cent) and additional individual skill training was given to clients. However, that was no difference between clients who had been given skill training and those who had not in the number of new skills acquired during the experimental period.

Following Porterfield and Blunden's work, a variety of researchers experimented with the implementation of Room Management in a variety of settings for people with SLDs (eg Coles and Blunden, 1979; Mansell, Felce, DeKock and Jenkins, 1982; Crisp and Sturmey, 1984; Pope, 1988). In most cases the dramatic increases in client engagement which occurred in the original study were not replicated, although substantial changes did occur. These studies show that Room Management is a flexible form of organisation which can be adapted to a variety of situations, for example: hospital day rooms, adult training centres, classrooms.

Additionally, a comparison of Room Management with small groups carried out by Sturmey and Crisp showed that Room Management resulted in greater overall client engagement.

Sturmey and Crisp also showed that the implementation of Room Management resulted in a reduction of these behaviours for a number of the people involved.

However, more detailed studies showed that this increased group engagement when Room Management was in force, was the result of only some of the clients involved being engaged for a greater proportion of time. The impact of Room Management was different for different clients; a study by Mansell et al (1982) found that clients fell into one of three groups: those who were already engaged for a high proportion for the time, those who were engaged only for a small proportion of the time before Room Management was introduced and had dramatically increased levels of engagement when Room Management was introduced, and those who were engaged for only a small proportion of the time whether or not Room Management was in place.

Mansell et al's study also showed that there was an association between the level of engagement achieved under Room Management and severity of disability. Those with the most profound learning difficulties were unlikely to be engaged for a significant amount of time under either Room Management or non-Room Management. Similarly, in a study of two classes for pupils with PMLDs, which were using Room Management for part of each day, we found that the less able pupils were engaged for less than 20 per cent of the time regardless of whether or not RM was in force (Ware and Evans, 1989).

These findings go some way to explain the comparatively low changes in group engagement in some studies. For example only a modest increase in the level of engagement (from 30 per cent to 44 per cent) was achieved when Room Management was introduced with a group of children who all had PMLDs (McBrien and Weightman, 1980).

Is Room Management then an inappropriate form of organisation for classes where all or some of the pupils have PMLDs? In terms of the extent to which pupils are engaged in meaningful activities Room Management seems to make least difference to those whose difficulties are so profound that they are engaged for only a small proportion of the time. However, our study, in addition to supporting the findings of Felce et al and McBrien and Weightman, showed that Room Management was successful in tackling another of the problems which arise when staff work with groups of people with severe and profound difficulties. In our study we found that adult attention was much more evenly divided between more and less able pupils when Room Management was in force. (More able pupils received twice as much adult attention as less able pupils during non-Room Management sessions, and only 5 per cent more when Room Management was operating). This more equal distribution of adult attention under Room Management is particularly important when we take into account that, while the less able children were only likely to be engaged for about 30 per cent of the time when they were receiving adult attention, their engagement fell to less than 10 per cent when they were not being attended to.

Evidence for the usefulness of Room Management in classes where pupils have a mixture of severe and profound learning difficulties comes from Pope's study (Pope, 1988). She found that overall engagement increased from 37.5 per cent to 69 per cent and that inappropriate behaviours and inactivity decreased. Although it is not possible to tell from her study the extent to which the more handicapped pupils were involved in these changes, Pope notes that informal observations suggested that all the pupils showed greater attention when Room

Management was in force. The results of her study and ours taken together suggest the Room Management is a useful form of organisation whether pupils with PMLDs are in separate classes or integrated into groups which also contain pupils with SLDs.

Although Room Management approaches have recently fallen into disfavour (eg Sebba et al, 1993), used flexibly they can ensure that all pupils have an opportunity for both group and individual work, especially in integrated classes. Basically what Room Management does is to provide a way of ensuring that those pupils who are not currently being directly taught are usefully engaged. This principle can be applied regardless of whether the direct teaching takes place on a group or an individual basis. Consequently, in a class catering for pupils with a wide range of severe and profound learning difficulties, a mixture of group and individual teaching can be arranged according to the needs of the pupils and the aims of particular activities.

The research reported in this chapter not only suggests that the adoption of a room management type procedure may be advantageous in classes where some or all of the pupils have PMLDs; it also has wider implications for classroom organisation. The same form of classroom organisation is not necessarily suitable for all activities, and different forms of organisation may be required to achieve the same results with different pupils. Overall, in order for classroom organisation to be effective, aims and priorities need to be clearly specified, and the organisation adopted to achieve them needs to be carefully and regularly evaluated.

CHAPTER SEVEN

Using Interaction in the Education of Pupils with PMLDs (i) Creating Contingency-sensitive Environments

Jean Ware

My interest in the role of interaction in the education of children with PMLDs comes originally from the view that what we should be concerned to do when we work with people with PMLDs is to enable them to participate as far as possible in all that happens to them (eg Williams, 1978; Porterfield, 1982). This view is supported by the work of the philosopher of Aspin (1982); Aspin stresses the importance of interaction in the education and development of all human beings.

In our initial investigations in this area we found that on the whole pupils with PMLDs had few opportunities for interaction of any sort, and even fewer which gave them the opportunity to participate (Ware, 1987; Ware and Evans, 1986). For example, in four classes for pupils with PMLDs where we studied the staff-pupil interactions in some depth, we found that the majority of interactions were extremely brief, lasting less than one minute each, and that interactions occurred on average only once every 12–13 minutes (Ware, 1990). Additionally, there was wide variation between pupils in the extent to which the adults initiating an interaction behaved as if they expected a response from the pupil, with those pupils who had more severe disabilities being less likely to receive initiations which expected a response. Adults rarely responded to pupils' behaviours or gave the pupil the opportunity to take the lead in interaction. (On average less than 10 per cent of pupils' behaviours were responded to, although staff were much more likely to respond to vocalisations than to other behaviours, suggesting that they may be discriminating in favour of behaviours which appear to have the potential for communication).

In that our findings closely paralleled both those of researchers examining interactions between staff and people with severe and profound learning difficulties in other environments, and those investigating interactions of caregivers with infants with severe physical and intellectual handicaps, they were not unexpected, and nor do they reflect adversely on the classroom staff involved. Nonetheless, they give a rather bleak picture of the interactive environment experienced by pupils with PMLDs. However there were also large differences between staff in the way they interacted with pupils, which suggested that it might be possible for staff to change their interactive behaviour.

My view that there was an urgent need to examine whether the types of interactions which pupils with PMLDs experienced in school could be affected by staff training, and whether this in turn would have an effect on the pupils' progress was strongly supported by an increasing volume of evidence from the field of mother-infant interaction.

Researchers in this field were gathering a mass of evidence which pointed to the importance of early interaction in the development of social, communication and cognitive skills in both handicapped and non-handicapped infants. (For a recent review see Mitchell, 1987). This research shows that, long before the infant has any intention to communicate (in the sense of acting with a deliberate intention to affect someone else's behaviour) adults treat him or her *as if* their actions had meaning. The evidence also suggests that it is through this the infant learns to communicate (eg Scoville, 1984). Of particular importance to the interactive environment in the classroom is the evidence that infants who experience a more responsive environment make faster social and cognitive progress. For example, Lewis and Coates (1980) in a study of twelve week-old infants found an association between the mothers' responsiveness and the infants' cognitive development. They also report that similar associations have been found by other researchers. Of course, these findings do not prove that the mother's responsiveness causes the infant's cognitive gains, it might be that mothers are more responsive to infants who are cognitively advanced.

However, a study by Anderson and Sawin (1983) showed that a simple intervention procedure (having the mother present while a neonatal behaviour assessment was administered and explained) was successful in increasing mothers' responsiveness to their (non-handicapped) infants. The infants' responsiveness to their mothers also increased, and they were also more alert and showed more positive affect than infants whose mothers had not received the intervention, although they were only one month old. Anderson and Sawin suggest that the only possible explanation for this change in the infant's behaviour was that it resulted from the mother's increased awareness of how to respond to her infant.

Furthermore, research with infants with difficulties of various types and their caregivers, shows that not only do caregivers tend to be less responsive to their infants (and vice-versa), but that infants can make progress in communicative development when caregiver responsiveness is increased.

For example, Hanzlik and Stevenson (1986) found that mothers of infants with both cerebral palsy and learning disabilities demonstrated a higher overall level of behaviour, and a higher level of commands than mothers of infants without difficulties. This was true regardless of whether the infants with cerebral palsy were compared with others of the same chronological age (mean 21 months) or the same mental age (mean 11.6 months). The cerebral palsied infants, and another group of infants with moderate learning disabilities (but not cerebral palsy), had a lower overall level of behaviour than non-handicapped infants of the same chronological age, and they also engaged in fewer verbal interactions with their mothers. Additionally, the infants with disabilities were more likely to be involved in competing behaviour with their mothers than non-handicapped infants of either the same CA or the same MA.

Mahoney and Robenalt (1986), comparing the interactions of infants with and without handicaps with their mothers during free play, found that infants with Down's Syndrome (MA 15–19 months) 'were less active communicative partners' than a carefully matched group without disabilities. They also found that the mothers of the children with Down's Syndrome were more likely to dominate the interaction rather than mother and infant being more or less equal partners, as was the case with the non-disabled group. That is, the mothers of the Down's Syndrome infants took more turns, gave more commands, and spent less time responding to their children than the mothers of the non-handicapped group. Mahoney and Robenalt suggest that while it is likely that the mothers were attempting to elicit a greater amount of activity from their child by asking them to do things; this could well have been counter-productive, resulting in the child becoming less active.

Bray (1988) compared children with Down's Syndrome and severe learning difficulties aged between two and six years with two groups of children without disabilities (same chronological age and same mental age). She found that the children with Down's syndrome were less likely to be involved in interactions where they took the lead, or where the lead was equally shared between the partners, than children of the same chronological age. They were also less likely to experience equal interactions than children of the same mental age. Bray also found that the Down's Syndrome group were more likely to be involved in negative interaction and suggested that non-disabled children may stimulate their parents into appropriate forms of interaction whereas those with disabilities may not.

As in our classroom studies, the research also seems to show that the greater the severity of the infant's handicap the greater the problems are likely to be (eg Terdal, 1976; Cunningham et al, 1981).

A number of investigators have demonstrated that it is comparatively simple to intervene in interactions between caregivers and infants with difficulties to produce interactions which are both more satisfying for both partners and resemble those occurring between caregivers and those infants without difficulties who make most cognitive gains in the early months of life.

For example, McCollum (1984) worked with caregiver-infant pairs for whom social interaction had been identified as a problem area, including one pair where the infant had severe cerebral palsy. She demonstrates that an individualized intervention, the Social Interaction Assessment and Intervention, enabled caregivers to adjust their interactions in the direction of greater responsiveness. The change in caregiver behaviour resulted not only in increased infant participation in the interaction, but also in greater enjoyment for both partners.

Barrera, Rosenbaum and Cunningham (1986) conducted a particularly interesting study with pre-term babies and their parents. Their study compared two forms of intervention, one aimed mainly at parent-infant interaction, and the other aimed primarily at the infants' cognitive development, with two non-intervention groups, one of pre-term and one of fullterm infants. They found that both intervention groups made gains in cognitive development during the period of the study compared with the non-intervention group of pre-term infants, and that by the end of the study differences between the pre-term intervention groups and the fullterm group had disappeared. Of particular interest is their finding that the group who had the parent-infant intervention most closely resembled the fullterm group in the high levels of responsiveness of mothers to their infants, and in the extent to which they provided a variety of stimulation. Barrera et al suggest that the parent-infant intervention effectively 'normalises' the home environment. Like Bray (above) they suggest that, while normal healthy infants may stimulate their parents into providing experiences that foster development, the parents of infants with handicaps may need help to do this.

Mahoney and Powell, working with infants with moderate or severe disabilities and their parents, found that parents were in general very successful in implementing turn-taking strategies (waiting for the child to act first, imitating the child's behaviour, following the child's lead). Furthermore, implementation was associated with an increase in the responsiveness of the interactive environment the parents provided for their children, and with greater developmental gains for the children. However, for some parents there also seemed to be a negative effect in important areas such as warmth and enjoyment (Mahoney and Powell, 1988).

Given our evidence that staff in classes for pupils with PMLDs find difficulty in sustaining positive interactions with children who are unresponsive (Ware and Evans, 1986, 1987; Ware, 1987, 1990), it seemed likely that giving attention to the purpose, structure and effect of interaction would offer a fruitful source for the development of productive teaching strategies in PMLD classes. Furthermore, our evidence taken together with that from research into interactions between mothers and their handicapped infants suggested that it was reasonable to expect that special efforts would have to be made by adults interacting with children and young people with PMLDs to provide a contingency-sensitive environment, i.e. one which gave the child both opportunities to initiate and time to respond, and allowed them to take the lead in interactions.

Influence of inservice training of staff on the type of interactions experienced by pupils with PMLDs

We were, therefore, interested to see if comparatively simple training procedures could be used to help staff working with pupils with PMLDs to interact with them in ways which were likely to promote social and cognitive development. These training procedures were developed as part of a larger research project on the impact of the type of interactive environment provided in classes for pupils with PMLDs on the children's progress. The project was funded by the Economic and Social Research Council of Great Britain (under Grant No.R000 231239). Where our research differs from that of other investigators, who appear to have been thinking along very similar lines at the same time (eg Goldbart this volume, Watson this volume; Burford, 1988; Nind and Hewett, 1988; Goldbart, 1990) is that we have been concerned not with providing specific sessions of one-to-one 'interaction', but with all the interactions which go on in the normal course of a classroom day (during physiotherapy, drinks, and so on). We have therefore concentrated our efforts on the *structure* of interaction and not the content. Our contention is that pupils can be given time to respond regardless of the content of the interaction, which should be derived from normal curricular considerations.

This chapter has two purposes, first to report the findings of the research project, and second to look briefly at how these might be directly relevant to classroom teachers in their work with pupils with PMLDs.

The Contingency-sensitive Environments Research Project

The research was carried out in the PMLD classes of two London schools for children with severe learning difficulties. These classes catered for pupils with profound learning difficulties and additional handicaps such as motor and sensory impairments, although in one school they also contained individuals whose mental impairment was less severe but who had a multiplicity of other impairments, and one or two pupils who had profound learning difficulties without obvious additional impairments.

A total of thirty-eight children and approximately twenty-five adults were involved in the project in the two schools. They were observed over an eighteen month period using a schedule which measured children's and adults' interactive and communicative behaviour in order to assess the contingency-sensitiveness of the environment and children's responses to it. We felt it was important to collect data on each child individually because our previous research suggested that even within the same class different pupils might have very different interactive experiences. The observation schedule assessed adult initiations according to whether they allowed for and attended to possible responses from the child (ie were contingency-sensitive) and child responses as either positive, negative or nil. Child initiations and adult responses were also recorded. (See Table 7.1). Recording took place in real time using an Epson HX20 laptop computer, thus we were also able to preserve the sequence and duration of each interaction.

Staff training

After a period of baseline observation to assess the initial level of contingency-sensitive interactions, staff training interventions were made, first in School 1 and four months later in School 2, (ie a multiple baseline across settings) with the aim of changing adult behaviour in the direction of making the interactive environment more contingency-sensitive. The procedures used in the staff training programme were designed to incorporate the features suggested by Landesman-Dwyer

Table 7.1

TABLE 1

Definitions of Interactive and Communicative Behaviour

Adult Initiations		Child Initiations	
Type	**Definition**	**Type**	**Definition**
CONTINGENCY-SENSITIVE	Approaches child in such a way as to allow for a response from the child, eg. calls child by name and waits for head turn, arm raise, smile etc.	INTENTIONAL COMMUNICATION	eg. A child may reach out and touch you, look at you or may make eye contact. They may vocalize when you have just left them to deal with someone else.
		RESPONSE TO ENVIRONMENT	eg. Looks up when someone passes nearby, or when the door squeaks. Vocalizes when another child vocalizes, or in response to a particular member of staff speaking to another person. Smiles and look when the wind waves the leaves of a tree just outside the window.
		VOLUNTARY	eg. arm movements, leg movements, apparently random vocalizations.
		INVOLUNTARY	Coughs, sneezes, yawns, fits.
NOT CONTINGENCY-SENSITIVE	Approaches child in such a way as not to give child opportunity to make a response eg. moves child without speaking first and waiting for a response	PURPOSEFUL	eg. playing with a toy, walking, picking up a piece of equipment
		STEREOTYPY	Those repetitive behaviours which some children show, rubbing, banging repeated movements.
		EATING AND DRINKING	
Child Responses		**Adult Responses**	
POSITIVE	When adult has approached child (regardless of type of approach) and the child changes behaviour, eg. smiles, makes eye contact with adult, vocalises etc. or, when adult comments about play activity, continues to engage in that activity (see above). All behaviourial changes count as positive responses unless unambiguously negative (see below).	POSITIVE CONTINGENT	Response from an adult which is clearly contingent on what the child has just done eg. 'good boy' or remark accompanied by child's name, in response to action or vocalisation; response which encourages child to continue action eg. "That's right, you ring the bell".

Table 1 *(Continued)*

TABLE 1			
Definitions of Interactive and Communicative Behaviour			
Adult Responses		**Child Responses**	
Type	**Definition**	**Type**	**Definition**
NEGATIVE	Child responds to adult approach by a change in behaviour but the change is deliberately and unambiguously negative eg. pushes adult or proffered toy away; actively resists adult's efforts to move or dress him/her etc.	NEGATIVE CONTINGENT	Responds to child in a way which discourages child from continuing action eg. removes toy; says "Don't do that" etc. but response is still clearly contingent on child's behaviour.
NONE	When adult has approached child (regardless of type of adult approach) and the child's behaviour is not observed to change in any way. *Unless* the adult addresses the child in such a way that a continuation of previous behaviour appears as a response eg. child playing with toy – adult says "That's right, you make it go" – child continuing playing counts as a response.	NONE	No response from adult before a child commences a new behaviour.

and Knowles (1987) as being important for the effectiveness of training, i.e.:

(1) Short Sessions.

(2) Time for practice between sessions.

(3) Direct relevance to the staff in each school by use of verbal and video examples of their own interactions with pupils.

(4) General positive feedback on performance.

(5) Personal and specific positive feedback to each individual member of staff combined with suggestions on how to improve their own performance.

Training began with adult initiations since we hypothesised that these would be easier for adults to change, and then progressed to adult responses to children's initiations and finally to allowing the child to take the lead in interactions. (Multiple Baseline across behaviours). The training sessions were provided during the school day so that all those who worked regularly with the children (teachers, assistants, therapists, nurses) could attend. Feedback to staff continued after the training was complete in order to maintain increases in contingency-sensitiveness.

Observation was continued for a further period after feedback was discontinued to assess the durability of changes in the absence of positive monitoring (four months in School 1 and five months in School 2).

Results and discussion

A number of unforeseen factors meant that the original multiple baseline design had to be modified during the course of the project. Chief amongst these was high staff turnover in the classes where the project took place. This necessitated additional baseline and intervention phases at both schools (in order to gather baseline data on new staff, and train them in the provision of a highly contingency-sensitive environment). Additionally, in School 2, the therapists and nurse opted not to attend the training sessions because they took place at times when they would otherwise be treating children. These difficulties highlight some of the problems in providing a consistently contingency-sensitive environment within a school setting. In the context of the project both these circumstances enabled us to make useful comparisons between trained and untrained staff.

Interestingly, staff in School 1 who had taken part in the first set of training sessions requested inclusion in the second set (which were primarily provided for new staff).

Adult initiated interactions

Our previous work suggests that there are likely to be differences between individual adults and children in the extent to which they make or receive initiations which allow for a response and that such initiations are less likely to occur in some activities than in others (Ware and Evans 1986). The impact of the staff training intervention on individual children and staff is therefore a crucial issue. Additionally, given our concern with the general classroom environment, the extent to which contingency-sensitive initiations occurred across curriculum areas was also of interest to us.

Furthermore, there is some evidence, both from our own previous work (Ware and Evans, 1987; Ware, 1990) and that of others (eg Felce, 1991), that organization affects interaction. We might expect therefore that there would be differences at a school or classroom level, in the extent to which the intervention effects a change in the level of contingency-sensitive initiations.

Adult-initiated interactions were classified according to the extent that they included contingency-sensitive initiations as: very low (<20%), low (20–39.9%), moderate (40–59.9%), high (60–79.9%), or very high (80% +).

Individual children

Of the 38 children who were observed at some point there was sufficient data for analysis at an individual level on the interactions experienced by only 29 (two children died, four moved away, two were very irregular attenders and one joined towards the end of the project).

Typically, individual children in both schools received highly variable levels of contingency-sensitive initiations prior to the training; as illustrated by the three examples in Figures 7.1a, 1b and 1c. However, there were also differences in levels between children, with those in School 2 generally receiving on average a low or moderate level, while some children in School 1 (generally those who were more able) received a high or very high level. During the course of the intervention children in both schools typically experienced increased and more consistent levels of contingency-sensitive initiations (see Figure 7.1), with 16 of the 17 children in School 1 and 6 of the 12 children in School 2 receiving either high or very high levels. This change was statistically significant (McNemar's test for the significance of changes = 5.81 $p<0.01$).

Not surprisingly there were some exceptions to this general pattern. Two children (both from one class in School 2) continued to receive low levels of contingency-sensitive initiations throughout the study. These children were both in one class in School 2 which had three teachers during the course of the study. Four children in School 1 received lower levels of contingency-sensitive initiations after staff training commenced than during baseline. However this needs to be seen in the context of all but one of the children in School 1 receiving high or very high levels even before the intervention commenced.

Individual adults

Before the staff training intervention took place, there was a high level of variability between individual adults in the extent to which they made initiations which gave the child a chance to respond, with some already showing a generally high and fairly consistent level of contingency-sensitive initiations (eg Figure 7.2a). Others were highly variable in their level of such initiations (eg Figure 7.2b). Clearly the teacher whose initiations are shown in Figure 7.2b was capable of interactions which

Figure 7.1a: Contingency-sensitive initiations received by individual children Celia, (School 1)

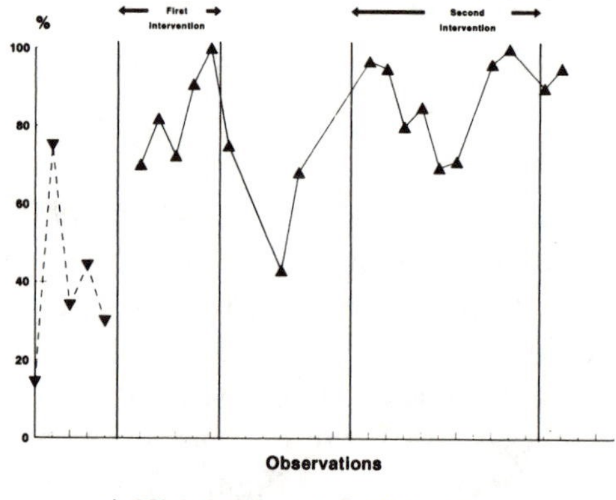

Figure 7.1b: Contingency-sensitive initiatives received by individual children Max, (School 2)

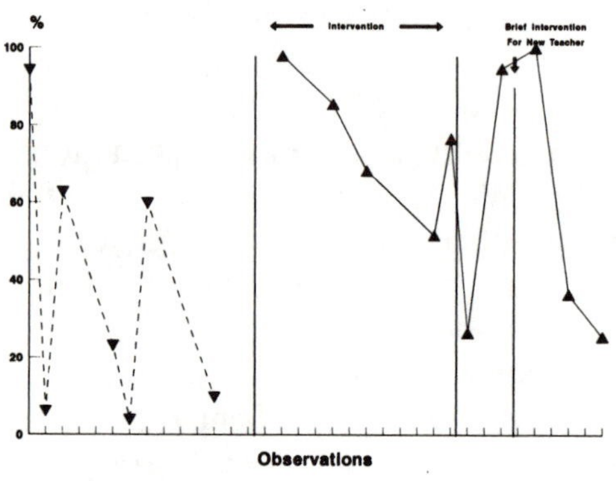

Figure 7.1c: Contingency-sensitive initiations received by individual children Alonso, (School 2)

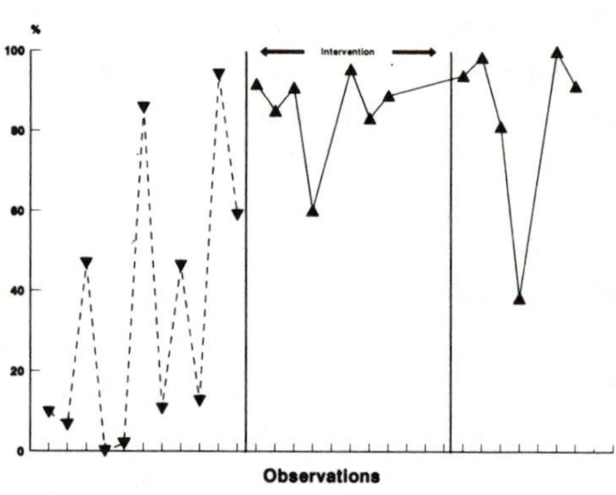

Figure 7.2a: Contingency-sensitive initiations made by adults: initially high adult

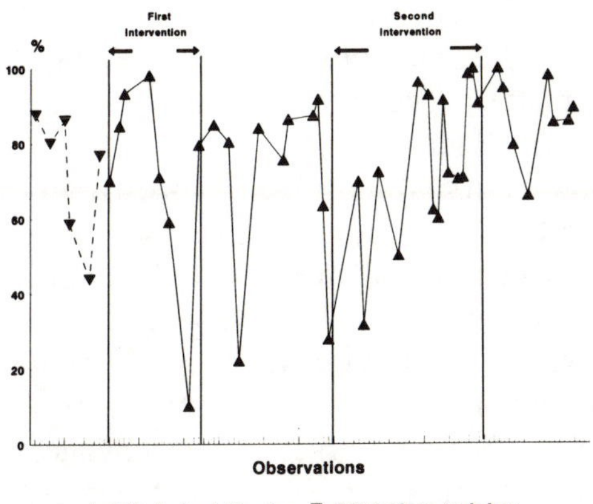

Figure 7.2b: Contingency-sensitive initiations made by adults: initially very variable adult

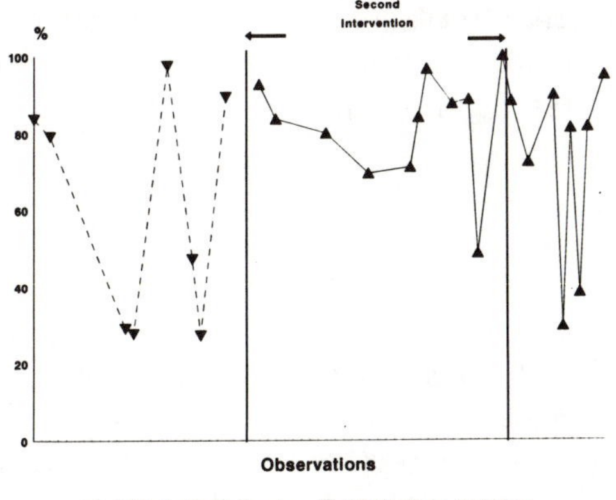

Figure 7.2c: Contingency-sensitive initiations made by adults: initially low adult

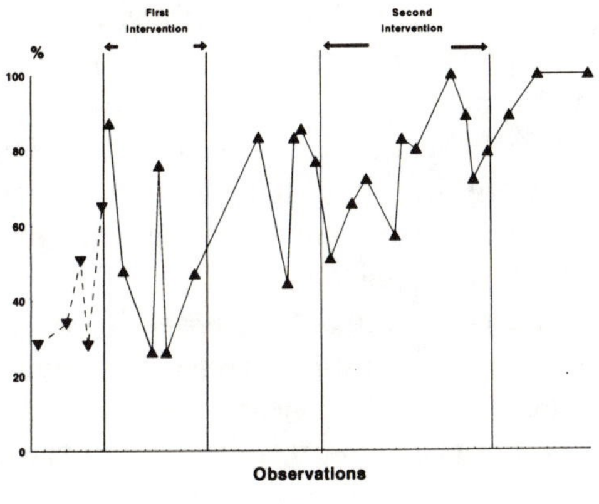

(in terms of her own initiations) were highly contingency-sensitive, but she did not consistently engage in such interactions. Finally there were those (a majority in School 2, but comparatively few in School 1) who, during baseline made a generally low level of contingency-sensitive initiations (eg Figure 7.2c).

During the intervention(s) most staff moved to a high and generally consistent level of contingency-sensitive initiations, with the most frequent pattern being that shown in Figure 7.2c. This suggests that the training intervention was most effective with those staff who initially provided the lowest levels of contingency-sensitive initiations, and that the general increase in levels of contingency-sensitive initiations during and after the intervention was largely due to changes in the patterns of interaction provided by these staff. Additional evidence that it was the intervention which effected the increase in the contingency-sensitiveness of adult initiations comes from the fact that staff who did not attend the training sessions (either because they were not regular classroom staff, or because they joined the staff after the intervention began) did not show an increase (eg Figure 7.3).

Curriculum areas

The picture of initiations across curriculum areas is complicated by the variability between children and adults. Additionally, since we observed children in rotation, the amount of data available on different curriculum areas is very variable, with only those activities which took place on a frequent basis (eg physiotherapy, language, drinks, individual work) providing sufficient data for any definite conclusions to be drawn. However, the data available does suggest that the overall picture is not simply a result of dramatic improvements in one curriculum area but, as with individual adults, the result of an increase in consistency during and after the intervention both within and between curriculum areas in the extent to which initiations were contingency-sensitive. The types of changes which occurred within curriculum areas once training began are shown in Figure 7.4. Examination of Figure 7.4 shows that, once training began, the percentage of contingency-initiations generally increased and the variability between individual adults and children decreased in both schools. However, as overall levels of contingency-sensitive initiations fell once the training was completed, it also suggests that the impact of the training was relatively short-lived, at least on the first occasion that training took place (see below).

Figure 7.3: Contingency-sensitive initiations made by therapist who did not attend training

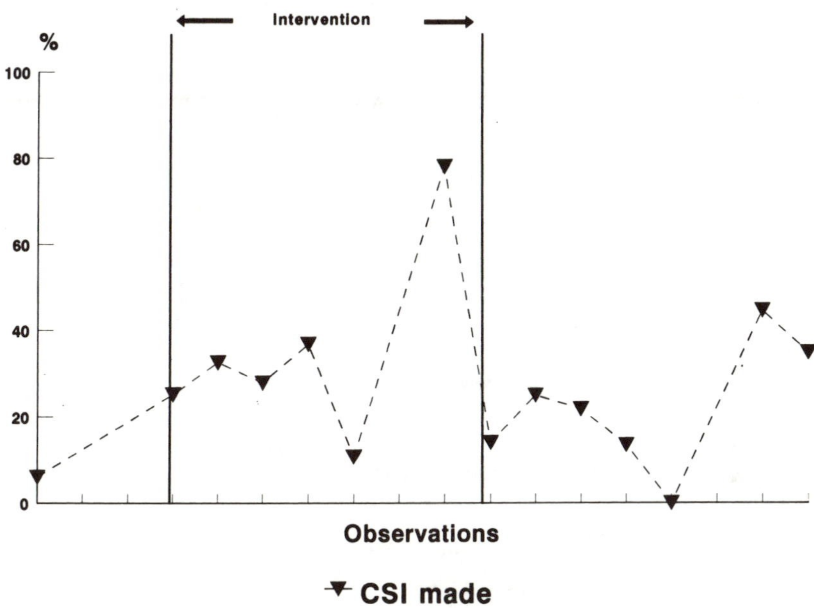

Overall results for School 1 and School 2

Overall, as can be seen from Figure 7.5, in both schools the level of contingency-sensitive adult initiations increased during the training interventions. Additionally, even though the data in Figure 7.5 consists of percentages averaged across children, there is also a decrease in variability, thus the intervention was successful to some extent in providing an environment which was consistently contingency-sensitive. These were generally reflected in the behaviour of individual adults, the experience of individual children and across curriculum areas. However, it is clear from Figure 7.5 that there were also differences between the two schools. In School 1 the average level of contingency-sensitive initiations was already comparatively high before the training intervention took place; nonetheless, especially during the second intervention, there is an overall increase in mean levels (from about 65 per cent to about 80 per cent). In School 2, by contrast, the average level of contingency-sensitive initiations was low and very variable before the intervention, and the increase during the intervention was very marked, (from about 40 per cent to about 70 per cent), although in fact the post intervention level of contingency-sensitive initiations was higher in

Figure 7.4a (Part One): Contingency-sensitive initiations – curriculum areas. Drinks School 1

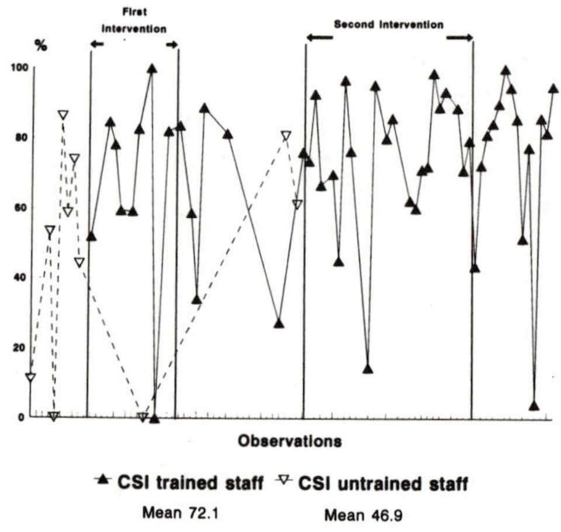

Figure 7.4a (Part Two): Contingency-sensitive initiations – curriculum areas. Drinks School 2

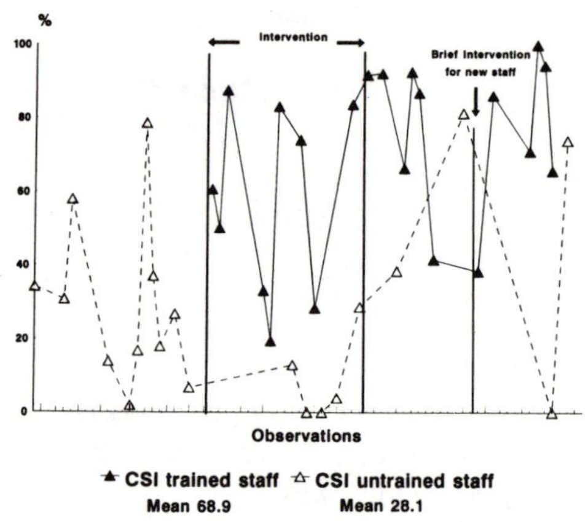

School 1. Additionally, there appear to be differences in the extent to which the increases in contingency-sensitiveness were maintained after the intervention, which are also evident in Figure 7.5.

The difference between the schools in levels of contingency-sensitive initiations before and during the intervention is probably accounted for partly by School 1 having a larger number of staff who originally showed high levels of contingency-sensitive initiations, perhaps because they were in general better qualified; but it may also have been partly an indirect result of the very different types of organisation in the two schools. In School 1 the PMLD classes were organised as a unit with a

Figure 7.4b (part one): Contingency-sensitive initiations – curriculum areas. Physiotherapy, School 1

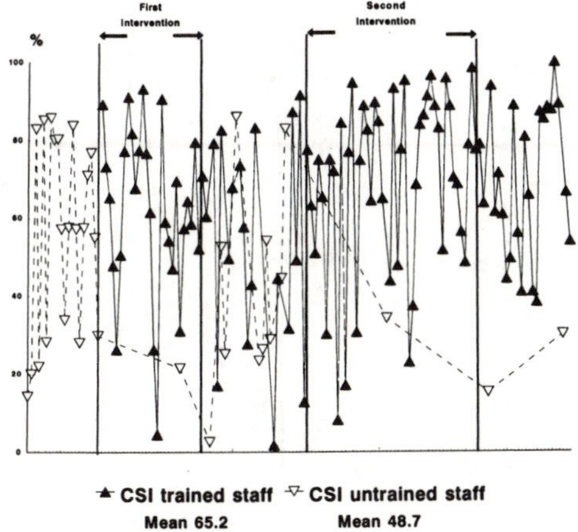

Figure 7.4b (part two): Contingency-sensitive initiations – curriculum areas. Physiotherapy. School 2

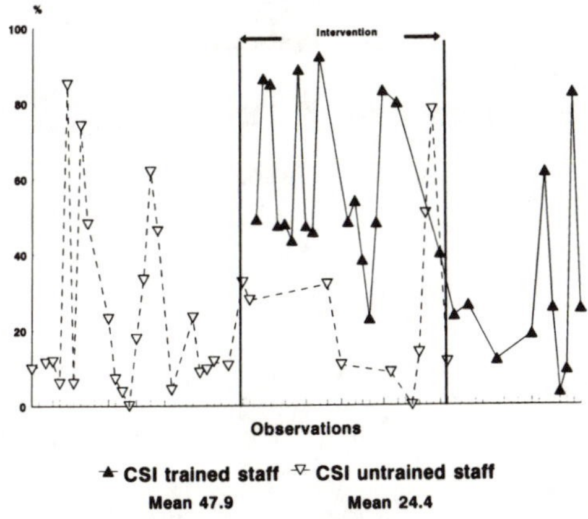

teacher-in-charge, a highly structured timetable and a well-developed system of recording.

By contrast School 2 had made an effort to integrate the two PMLD classes into the remainder of the school, with one being placed in each of the senior and junior teams. In practice this meant that these two classes functioned largely autonomously and both had a less pronounced degree of structure than that evident in School 1. A further factor was probably the fact that one class in School 2 had three different teachers during the course of the project. It was in this class that two children did not experience any increase in initially low levels of contingency-sensitive initiations. Additionally, in School 2, therapy

Figure 7.5a: Contingency-sensitive initiations. Data point means (i.e. average percentage of CSI in each data point). School 1

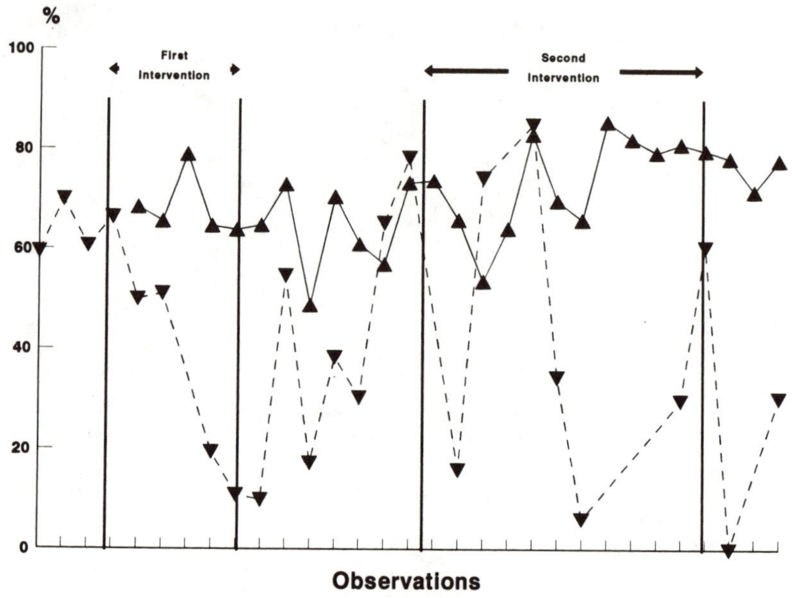

Figure 7.5b: Contingency-sensitive initiations. School 2

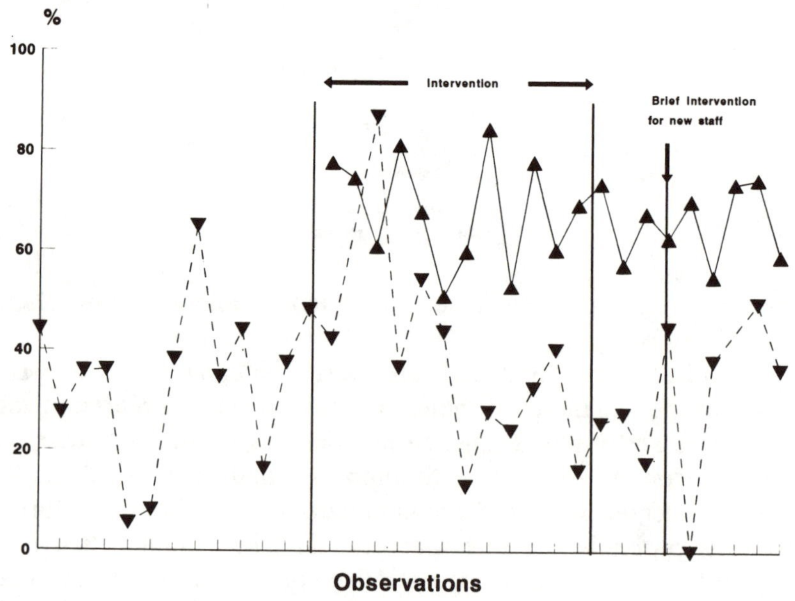

staff opted not to attend the training sessions and, because the training sessions were provided in teaching time, other staff who worked in the PMLD classes on a part-time basis were unable to attend.

The difference in the extent to which the increases were maintained after the intervention could have resulted from the interaction of several factors. In School 2 there were sometimes problems with the technical equipment for training, making it difficult to provide detailed and specific feedback on staff performance. Staff in School 1 who were present throughout the project took part in two training interventions whereas, when training was provided for full-time classroom staff who had joined during the course of the project in School 2, it was carried out on three half days at weekly intervals giving little opportunity for practice or feedback; and there was no opportunity for other staff to use it as a 'refresher course'. One teacher and one assistant took part in that intervention. The contribution of this factor is supported by the fact that the level of contingency-sensitive initiations declined after the first intervention ended in School 1 as it did after the main intervention ended in School 2. Work on the impact of ecological factors on the effectiveness of training (Landesman-Dwyer and Knowles, 1987) would suggest that the fact that all relevant staff took part in training in School 1, but not in School 2 probably also contributed to this difference.

Pupil initiated interactions

Adult responses to child initiations

Once overall levels of contingency-sensitive initiations showed an increase, the focus of training was switched to adult responses to children's initiations. Unfortunately, problems with the computer analysis of the data meant that it was not possible to provide staff with such detailed feedback on their performance for this aspect of the contingency-sensitive environment; however, positive video examples were used combined with detailed discussion of each child's behaviours and their communicative significance.

Our previous work and that of other researchers suggests that adult responses to children's behaviours would initially be at a low level. Analysis of the data showed that this was indeed the case, with staff responding to pupils on average only about 10 per cent of the time they were interacting with them in School 1 and 8 per cent of the time in School 2.

Examination of Table 7.2 suggests that the staff training intervention had little positive effect on overall levels of staff responding; indeed the

Table 7.2: Mean levels of adult responses (as % of interaction time) in schools 1 and 2

	Baseline	Intervention 1	Maintenance /Baseline 2	Intervention 2	Maintenance 2
School 1	10.49	7.45	7.05	8.50	8.18
	Baseline 1	Baseline 2	Baseline 3	Intervention	Maintenance
School 2	10.20	3.84	8.97	10.23	8.30

fact that staff responding to children's initiations dropped in both the first intervention in School 1 and the second baseline in School 2 suggests that extraneous factors (such as the time of year, or forthcoming staff departures) may have had more influence than the staff training. Several aspects of the staff training procedure could have contributed to this lack of impact. The lack of detailed specific feedback on staff responses may well have been a contributory factor, as may the order in which initiations and responses were dealt with during the training. Adults' concentration on changing their own initiations may have disrupted their normal patterns of responding. Additionally, our initial hypothesis that adults would find it easier to alter their initiations than their responses appears to have been correct, and this combined with the other factors might well have resulted in the lack of positive effect from the training. It is possible that staff training would have been more effective overall if responses had been dealt with first rather than initiations.

Individual children

On a more positive note, this overall result masks important differences between individual pupils. Particularly during the second intervention in School 1, there was less variability between pupils in the extent to which they received adult responses to their initiations than during the baseline. This reduction in variability resulted both from those pupils who had received the highest levels of response experiencing decreased levels and those who had received least responses experiencing increased levels. Additionally, adults were more likely to respond to communicative behaviours after the intervention.

Our lack of success in changing the extent to which adults responded to children's initiations contrasts with the success reported in studies of carers and infants with difficulties (see above). The most likely explanation for this difference seems to be that they were working with individual carer-infant pairs whereas we were concerned with general classroom interactions.

Opportunities to take the lead in interaction

There was little evidence of any overall change in the opportunities given to pupils to take the lead in interactions, arguably an important step in the development of interactive competence.

Influence of the contingency-sensitiveness of the environment on pupil progress

Any discussion of progress in relation to people with PMLDs is fraught with difficulties (see Chapter 1, this volume). However, the research discussed at the beginning of this chapter suggests that the development of interactive skills underpins progress in a range of other areas. Thus increasingly mature patterns of participation in interaction – more varied and sophisticated initiations and responses and the development of equal partnerships in interaction – could be seen as preliminary evidence for progress.

Responses to adult initiations

Because the staff training was limited in its impact, affecting mainly the way in which adults initiated interactions with children, it would be unreasonable to expect wide-ranging effects on the pupils' progress. However, examining changes in the children's patterns of participation in interaction over the duration of the project shows that there were some developments towards greater maturity.

In particular, there was clear progress in the extent to which children responded to adult initiations during the course of the project. As can be seen from Figure 7.6, the extent to which children make positive responses to adult initiations generally follows the pattern of contingency-sensitive initiations quite closely and there is also a gradual upward trend after the intervention. In School 1 (Figure 7.6a), this effect is quite clear, with the increase in child responding lagging slightly behind the increase in contingency-sensitive initiations from adults. The results for School 2 (Figure 7.6b) are more equivocal. Although there is a clear rise and a continuing upward trend during the intervention, there is also evidence of an upwards trend during baseline which does not correspond to the level of contingency-sensitive initiations. This is difficult to explain, although there were changes in both children and

Figure 7.6a: Children's positive responses and adult contingency-sensitive initiations. Data point means (Average percentage of CSI in each data point). School 1

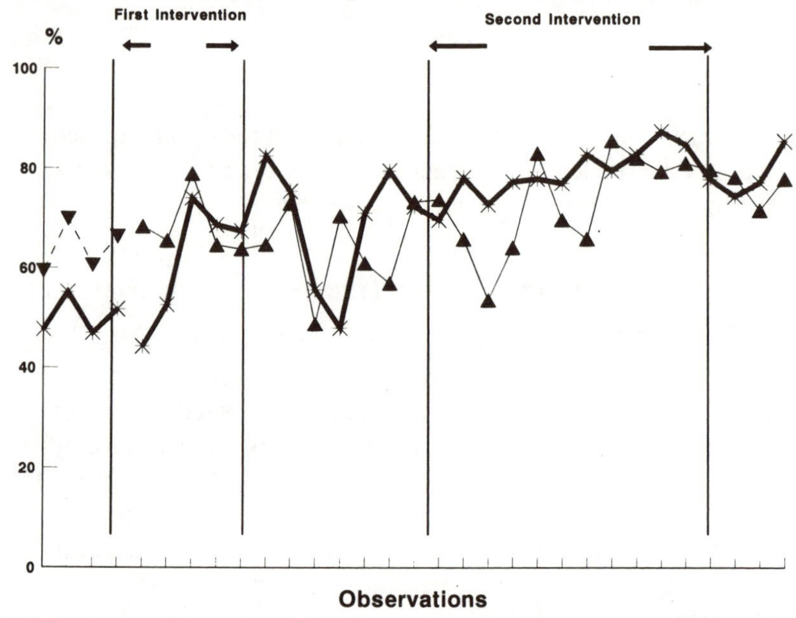

Figure 7.6b: Children's positive responses and adult contingency-sensitive initiations. Data point means (Average percentage of CSI in each data point). School 2

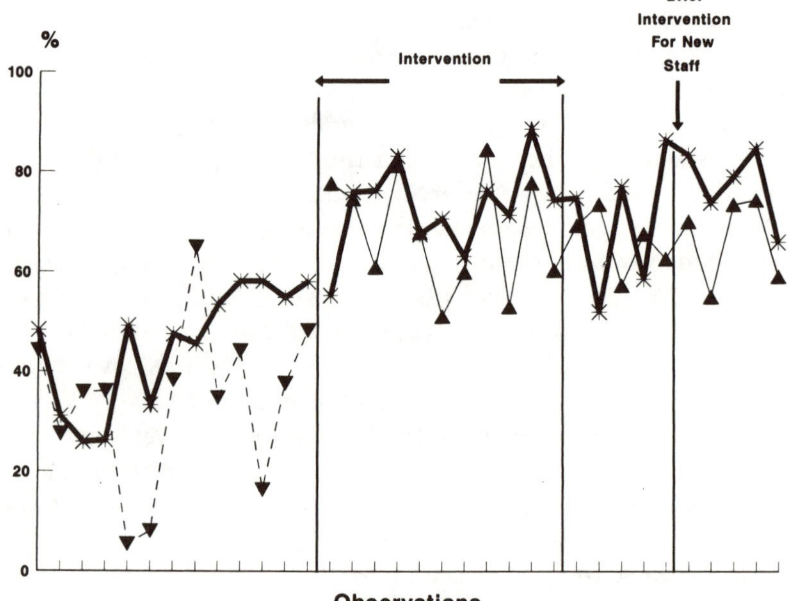

staff in both classes in School 2 at about this point in the baseline observations with the deaths of two of the children, and the appointment of two new teachers. However, the fact that this increase in child responses levels off towards the end of the baseline phase enables us to be reasonably confident that the increase in positive responses during the intervention relates to the increase in adult contingency-sensitive initiations.

This overall pattern is generally reflected in the data for individual children. For example, Celia, for whom the data on adult initiations was given in Figure 7.1a shows a highly variable pattern of responses throughout the project (see Figure 7.7). But these responses also generally reflect the level of contingency-sensitive initiations she received and show an upward trend, especially during the second intervention.

Child Initiations

A preliminary analysis of child initiations shows that, while in absolute terms changes in behaviour were small, in general the children seemed to change their behaviour in ways which indicated progress. For one child, for example, the number of times she was observed to be inactive reduced by one third, and the number of times she reacted to environmental stimuli increased threefold. For another child, periods of inactivity reduced to zero and reactions to environmental stimuli increased by 25 per cent, while intentional communications doubled (See Table 7.1 for definitions).

Our view that these changes in interactive behaviour represent progress for these very handicapped children is supported by data from staff interviews. In both schools staff reported that children were more responsive and more enjoyable to be with after the intervention. They also noticed that at least some children were developing more sophisticated initiations and saw this as significant progress.

Conclusions and implications

The results of this project show that the type of interactive environment experienced by pupils with PMLDs can be influenced to at least some extent by inservice training of staff, and that there is some evidence of enhanced pupil progress as a result.

Although the limited success of the staff training intervention meant that we were unable to assess the impact on pupils with PMLDs of an interactive environment which was contingency-sensitive in all three

Figure 7.7: Positive responses – individual child. Celia, School 1

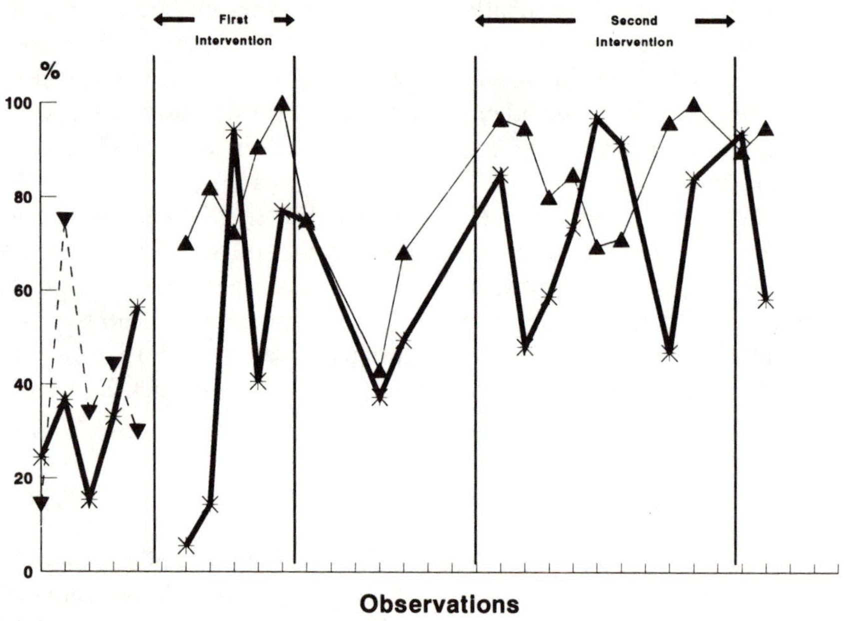

aspects, it did enable us to identify more clearly the factors influencing the success of the training. In particular, positive feedback emerged as a major factor in the success of the intervention in influencing interactive patterns in both the immediate and longer term. Additionally it seems possible that attempts to increase staff responses to children's initiations could be more successful if individual child-staff pairs were targeted initially, and then generalised to overall classroom practice.

There are three main implications of these findings for those who work with children with profound and multiple learning difficulties. First, positive monitoring has an important, if not a crucial, role to play in ensuring that children with PMLDs experience interactions which facilitate their development. Second, further research is required to find ways of carrying out this monitoring in ways which are less time intensive than the extensive data collection and analysis used in this project. Finally, organizational factors at both a school and classroom level play an important part in ensuring that an appropriate interactive environment is provided for pupils with PMLDs and this needs to be taken into consideration in the organization of provision and in staff and volunteer deployment. Opportunities for all staff to engage in training together are particularly important, as is training which is specific to the pupils they are working with. It is rare for either of these conditions to be met in school inservice training.

We are well on the way to being able to train staff to provide a contingency-sensitive environment for children with PMLDs, but unless we provide the conditions in which those skills can be exercised effectively the children will not benefit fully.

CHAPTER EIGHT

Using Interaction in the Education of pupils with PMLDs (ii) Intensive Interaction : Two Case Studies

Judith Watson

Introduction

This chapter describes a study of intensive interactive teaching at a school for pupils with severe or very severe learning difficulties, many of them with additional physical or sensory impairments. The background to the school's adoption of intensive interaction techniques is described by the then Assistant Head Teacher:

> Like most schools for pupils with very severe learning difficulties, Gogarburn School had developed a curricular approach in which skills learning, self help, table top and communication skills were predominant. Programmes were developed on pupils' needs as perceived by staff and parents. But the feeling grew that the pupils' day was becoming predictable and repetitive. Some pupils were working on skills that they would clearly never master to a satisfying degree, and which did not seem to have, for them, any intrinsic satisfaction. Many pupils seemed to spend an inordinate amount of time on table top activities of dubious educational value. The importance of emotional and social development was recognised, but was not necessarily seen as a central activity.
>
> In this curriculum model we are trying to analyze the skills used in infant-parent interaction and apply them to our situation. It does not mean treating our pupils like babies. It is very important to respect their chronological age, and to recognise that their life experience is very different from that of babies. However in order to give them the best possible opportunity to develop, and to facilitate the best communication they are capable of, we have to use all methods at our disposal, and this is one which seems to work.
>
> **Intensive interaction** consists of a member of staff working one-to-one with a pupil, concentrating all their attention on that pupil, and initially

> observing, and responding to, any movement, expression or sound given by the pupil. The member of staff is not *teaching* in a traditional sense, but responding creatively to the pupil. In doing so she will often use techniques which are part of parent-child interaction. Gradually games and sequences will emerge which the staff member will use and expand. The purpose of the games is to build a communicative relationship, and in so doing promote such things as pupil initiatives, eye-contact, turn-taking, understanding of cause and effect. Underlying all activities is the recognition of the importance of the pupil being an active partner in the engagement, consciously trying to move from the pupil as passive, and staff member active paradigm. (Knight and Watson, 1990).

In adopting this model the school have been greatly stimulated and helped by the work of movement therapists (Burford, 1990) and school staff at Harperbury Hospital School (Nind and Hewett, 1988; Hewett, 1989).

Senior school staff invited the present author to conduct an evaluation of intensive interactive teaching within the school for two reasons. First, they wished to see whether a study over the school year would produce evidence that the method was 'working' as they believed it was, and secondly, they felt that evaluation would help them to decide where to go next in developing their curriculum.

The time available to the researcher was, at most, one day weekly. Six pupils were chosen to represent a range of age and ability levels, and six members of staff agreed to participate by working with a given pupil over the period of study. Video recordings of interactive sessions were planned for each pupil-staff pair at approximately six-weekly intervals, and the nature, duration and location of each session was to be at the discretion of the member of staff concerned. After each videotaped session the member of staff was asked to complete an interaction record form, describing the 'best', 'worst', and any novel parts, and finally evaluating the session as a whole.

The video recordings thus obtained contain much rich data. Analysis so far has concentrated on communication, attention, and play with objects. The general conclusion is that intensive interaction sessions appear to facilitate developments in these and in other areas, probably because staff were able to observe pupils accurately and to respond to them sensitively during relatively short periods of concentrated 'engagement'.

Table 8.1 summarises the main features of the study, details of which are of course available in the main report (Knight and Watson, 1990).

Table 8.1: Main features of interactive study of six pupils

Pupil	**Residence**	**Notes on Early Progress**	**Notes from 1989 School Report**
B (M) 10 years	Home	Premature birth. Meningitis at 3 days. Epilepsy.	Has made progress in self help but requires constant supervision. No awareness of danger – investigates flexes, plugs etc, with his mouth.
R (M) 12 years Ross	Residential Care	Very severe learning difficulties of unknown cause. Epilepsy. Severe behaviour difficulties. He can be stubborn, disruptive and uncooperative	Speech improves slowly but noticeably. He will use single words as requests and is being taught a few Makaton signs. A happy boy but spends a lot of time in a world of his own. Sometimes he just gazes into space and it can be almost impossible to gain his attention. At others he is happy and alert, full of fun, willing to play games.
A (F) 13 years	Foster Home	Microcephalic with congenital brain dysplasia. Profound learning difficulties and severe motor disabilities. Sociable and determined.	Continues to improve in cooperative and self help skills. Shows a high degree of curiosity in her surroundings and now responds actively and vocally to people. She can indicate when she wants privacy. She responds well to interactive play. Communications are developing. Most are expressions of interest, involvement and anticipation.
S (M) 15 years	Hospital	Epilepsy. Tuberous Scoliosis. Profound learning difficulties with very low frustration level. Isolated, aggressive, unpredictable, sometimes bizarre behaviour.	Much less isolated. A little less volatile and aggressive. More happy to be part of group. More ready to accept turn taking. Few fits in school. Appears to hallucinate at times. **(Special note.** In movement S has a definite sophisticated but clear set of gestures which communicate his feelings.)

Table 8.1: Main features of interactive study of six pupils

T (F) 15 years	Hospital	Epilepsy. Multiple disabilities and profound learning difficulty. Very little vision. Scoliosis. Totally dependent for all aspects of her care. She is lovable and responds with smiles and vocalisations.	Happy sociable personality. She responds to people she knows. She is more alert and holding her head up better.
J (M) 19 years Johnnie	Hospital	Epilepsy. Profound learning difficulties. Slight hearing loss. Nonambulant. Responds well to music and noises.	Less lively and alert this year with poor general health. Usually appears unaware of other pupils. Smiles to familiar noises and reaches out occasionally. Tires quickly and lacks stamina. Alert and responsive when well.

Illustrative Example I : Carol and Ross

In this chapter the focus is on two staff-pupil pairs, as space does not permit sufficient detail to be usefully given on all six pupils. The first nursery nurse is referred to as Carol, and the pupil as Ross for the purpose of this report. Carol was new to the classroom and had never worked with Ross before the first interaction session, which was videotaped.

Ross is by far the most able of the six pupils in the study, and at twelve, the second youngest. He lives in a residential home, visiting his parents alternate weekends. His epilepsy is well controlled by drugs, and he is physically agile. Reports over years describe him as having severe learning difficulties and challenging behaviour ('stubborn, disruptive, and unco-operative'). Reports also note, however, that he plays imaginatively, and is interested in cartoons and fantasy. His most recent school report indicated that his behaviour is very variable, 'sometimes it is impossible to gain his attention, at others he is alert, full of fun.'

Five sessions were recorded over a period of about six months, on average lasting eighteen minutes.

Carol decided from the beginning that Ross needed as distraction-free an environment as possible, only using his usual classroom when the other pupils were absent. On other occasions she chose to use the soft play area of an adjoining classroom.

Carol adopted a following, reflective role with Ross. She waited for him to initiate activities, choosing a toy for example. She often repeated back an utterance or other noise, and copied his physical gait and gestures. She concentrated on 'reading' his intentions, co-operating in joint actions initiated by him, and extending sequences of pretend play.

The present report focuses on two areas of Ross's behaviour: play and language.

Play

Sessions involving Ross were always energetic with many changes of position and activity. He frequently broke off an apparently enjoyable activity to attend to something else. The soft play area used for two sessions was novel, and stimulated pretend play of a kind not observed by staff before.

During the second session Ross repeatedly flung himself onto the soft, yielding floor, and then jumped up to look over the side, approximately every minute, but with a greater frequency in the first half of the session. During the fourth session he immediately launched into the same bedtime routine as had developed in session two, snoring, pulling the duvet over, getting a pretend drink for himself and Carol, and deciding when it was time to get up, all with great enjoyment.

Ross's difficulty in attending to any one activity in a sustained manner is illustrated by play with a stuffed toy horse. He climbed on, with Carol behind, neighed and rocked with great good humour, then abandoned it after less than one minute.

The physical environment of the play sessions had a strong influence, as the above illustration shows. Within the confined area of soft play, unable to run about the classroom, Ross's imagination was stimulated by the plastic floor and walls, the duvets, cushions and soft toys, his language and play activity were adapted accordingly and completely different from his usual classroom behaviour. He did not sustain these novel activities for long, but by the end of the period of study there were indications that he was beginning to extend and vary them.

It would be wrong to judge Ross's capacity for sustained play from his behaviour in the novel setting. The first session was held in his usual, but empty, classroom, and lasted 15 minutes. Carol began by attempting to interest Ross in two toys that she had chosen, and her initiative was completely ignored. He reacted by walking away and bringing a pair of identical balls from the toy cupboard, one of which he gave to Carol. Thence followed a series of imitation games, Carol following his actions with her ball, to which Ross responded with relaxed and alert enjoyment.

This interesting tendency for Ross to choose pairs of identical toys for parallel play was noticeable throughout. He only engaged in activities initiated by himself, but quite deliberately organised Carol's parallel participation, from which truly co-operative play was beginning to develop.

The third session was especially notable in this respect. During almost the whole of its 23 minute duration Ross's attention was engaged. At the sand tray he took out two identical trowels, and two identical tippers, and parallel play began, with him in the lead, tipping and filling, with Ross starting to count, and Carol continuing. At several points during this remarkable period of sustained activity, Ross seemed to be briefly distracted, but Carol was able to skilfully move in to extend the activity in an interesting new direction. In the latter part of the same session Ross was occupied for six minutes in using Carol's bunch of keys to attempt the opening of various cupboards and doors, with systematic persistence and a degree of ingenuity. Items of vocabulary such as 'pity', 'locked' emerged which had not been heard before. Carol's strategy was to stand nearby reflecting his actions, repeating and expanding slightly on his remarks, and making it clear that she shared the object of his attention.

The last recorded session included five minutes of truly co-operative play, again of a kind not seen before. As usual, Ross chose the toys, a large pull-along trolley containing plastic bricks. Carol sat in the trolley, and Ross pulled it along for a short space, before they both pulled it along together. Ross then took out some bricks, began by hitting those held by Carol, and the two then placed alternate blocks, with Ross skilfully rectifying a deliberate mistake by Carol and gesturing her out of the way, before demolishing the six-foot edifice. His co-operation did not stop there, for he complied agreeably with Carol's instruction to pick them up.

Language

During normal activities in rather a noisy classroom with many distractions, Ross's language was described as being repetitive, apparently without communicative function, nonsocial (rarely addressed to the other pupils), and consisting largely of phrases from television cartoons, often said by Ross in front of a large mirror. Stock phrases were 'you alright?' 'get me out of here' and 'peow!' It is therefore of particular interest to examine his use of language with the calmer, concentrated context of one-to-one interaction during which he is making the running. It seems likely that Ross's verbal communications will be optimal during such times, when Carol is specially tuned into his speech, which seems clearest when he is obviously attentive and involved.

While not all the verbalizations are intelligible on the videotapes, the majority are. They include many of the above stock phrases, often expressions that have been heard on television, such as 'timber!', 'fire!', 'help!'. These were common during boisterous play. Another group consists of phrases used entirely appropriately and sometimes heard for the first time in the interactive settings: 'night-night', 'wake up', 'cock-a-doodle-doo', and 'cup of tea?' and during play with bricks, 'one, two', 'okay, ready?', 'eight, nine'.

Ross's language is more focused during play activities involving toys, and more expressive during gross motor play. During the latter, odd words are often inserted which appear to be out of context, but may be evidence of his difficulty in sustaining attention, utterances like 'fire' on hearing the bell, and 'house' on seeing a picture on a wall, while engaged in other activities.

It is noticeable that the stereotyped phrases used during boisterous play are often accompanied by funny noises, mock crying, and laughter. He uses a great many expressive vocalisations like groans, gulps, grunts, and mock agony, used to highlight activities which are exciting to him. The dominant functions are requests, 'get the ball', and comments 'all wet', 'pity' and fillers, 'and now, now', 'okay?'

A fair amount of detail has been given here to support the claim that for this pupil, the five individual sessions, averaging 18 minutes, were effective in providing a context which facilitated Ross's communications, ability to concentrate, co-operative behaviour, pretend play, and play sequences.

Illustrative Example II : Sue and Johnnie

Johnnie at 19 was the oldest pupil in the school and one of the least able and least active. He had frequent fits and was reported before the study began to be less well and less alert than formerly.

Sue, a nursery nurse, had never worked with Johnnie before the first videotaped session, but she knew him quite well from general classroom activities : she usually conducted interaction sessions with Johnnie on a mat, or he sat in an armchair, in the usual noisy and normally distracting classroom. She claimed, and her behaviour supported her claim, to never find it difficult to concentrate during intensive interaction. Six sessions were recorded, over a period of seven months, and lasted on average twenty-six minutes.

At first Johnnie appeared to be more animated and alert when Sue introduced a toy than when simply interacting with her. When no toy was involved he often appeared to avoid Sue by turning his head away, and seemed frequently to be very sleepy, yawning almost continuously for long periods. His attention was caught by rattling sounds and particularly by a large metallic toy car whose wheels rattled and spun. Almost all his vocalisations during the first sessions accompanied movements of this car, which he typically held to his face and mouth, tipping it from side to side and inspecting it closely. He showed excitement when Sue ran or spun the car on the floor and they both crawled after it.

One development over time was the willingness to share attention to the car. During the first session Johnnie skilfully and repeatedly moved it away from Sue's outstretched hand. During the third session he allowed her to touch it while he held it and during the next session a simple sharing game involving running the car along the floor was developing.

During the fifth session Johnnie was unusually vocal, looked directly at Sue, and smiled, in marked contrast to his earlier avoiding behaviour when he had pushed her face away. The last recorded session was even more rewarding. During ten minutes, on six separate occasions Johnnie placed his arm on Sue's shoulder, raised himself to a kneeling position, was rocked to and fro, and then lowered himself. This novel series of movements was repeatedly facilitated by Sue's alteration of her own position. There was clear evidence here that social interaction was becoming much more enjoyable for Johnnie during the sessions of intensive interaction.

Sue rarely talked with Johnnie during interactions which did not involved a toy, except to say his name. She blew on his cheek, whistled, nuzzled his face, and touched it with her hands. When the toy car was the focus of his attention she talked much more, as in 'here we go', 'wheels', touching the car meanwhile. Johnnie himself often said 'eeh' when his attention was caught by the car and he always reached toward it. While holding it his actions tended to be fairly stereotyped side to side movements near his face. Sue was adept at joining in and extending these movements in a variety of ways.

Staff interview

After the last video recording, all six members of staff were asked for their views concerning the importance of intensive interaction. Carol's comments are of special interest here:

> I think it's very important. I've got to know him a lot better, and he's got to know me a lot better. He's even learnt my name, and that's a lot for him because he doesn't talk to them.

Asked how her interaction experience affected her behaviour with Ross during the rest of the school day, she said:

> We're more pally. Because we've got to know each other better he trusts me more than if we hadn't done it. For example, if he's wanting something done he'll come to me and say my name. He doesn't say anyone else's name.

It is important to stress again that the only intensive interaction experiences for Ross were the five videotaped sessions during the study.

Sue commented in similar vein concerning her relationship with Johnnie:

> I've really got to know him better, more as a companion. It has increased the relationship. For example, at snack in the afternoon it's a social occasion. When he has finished I find I'm leaning towards him, touching him, and he reaches over to me.

She also stressed that for her time during interaction never seemed to drag.

Follow up

Six months after the evaluation study was completed, Ross was said by his class teacher and by Carol to be relating better to other pupils in his class. He would, for example, sometimes hand one a toy. He was also continuing to extend his vocabulary, and would make specific verbal requests, instead of simply 'please'.

He is also reported to be more involved socially, less likely to shut himself off from his peers, acting out cartoon characters in front of a mirror. This had been common when noises and distractions had been at a high level. This year his class group is quieter, which, it is now appreciated, is very important for Ross. Both members of staff feel that interaction has enhanced and extended behaviour which was seen in class, by providing a less distracting and more responsive environment. They plan this year to encourage the development of play sequences and appropriate language during interaction sessions at least weekly.

Johnnie has left school and attends an Adult Training Centre.

The school policy on interaction continues to develop. Planned activity time for teachers is also attended by the nursery nurses and has the broad theme of communication. The general emphasis in school remains that of building up relationships using interaction as one means of doing this. The head teacher reports that the evaluation study helped boost staff morale in recognising what they were doing as important, and validated what they were doing.

Conclusion

All six pupils in the study made progress during the year in different ways. This can be generally said to be in the broad areas of communication, social awareness, and responsiveness. Comparisons between them are not particularly enlightening. Enjoyment of both staff member and pupil is the main feature of the videotapes that strikes the observer.

As noted, during the study, Johnnie became markedly more sociable, gaining pleasure from interaction and demonstrating this.

Ross as the most able of the six pupils, made progress most strikingly in his language (appropriate use and expanding vocabulary); interpersonal behaviour (co-operation and role play with another); attention; and extended sequences of pretend play. The powerful effect of the context has been shown, and the importance of choice and self initiated activity for Ross has been highlighted.

The videotapes provide evidence to school staff of Ross's abilities which has surprised them, and this can be used as a basis for planning ways of facilitating future development. These range from an enhanced awareness of his distractibility under certain conditions, to the development of play sequences in which he leads, with a staff member following in a sensitive, interested manner which enhances the likelihood of play activities being prolonged and made more complex.

McConkey, in a very accessible recent article (1990) concludes 'the challenge now is to refocus the play activity or interactive game through adding to it or by guiding the child's participation so that new skills can be brought in'. He also points out that 'preplanned blanket stimulation is much easier to provide in classrooms than is the intuitive, individual response of the successful interactor. It is sad that so much teacher education is still directed at advancing the former and neglects the latter.'

Schools such as the Scottish one which initiated the present study are finding that incorporating intensive interaction into their pupils' educational experience promises well for the future.

Bibliography

Aitken, S. (1988) Computer-aided instruction with the multiply impaired. *Journal of Mental Deficiency Research 32*, 257–263.

Alberto, P., Jobes, N., Sizemore, A. and Dorans, D.A. (1980) A comparison of individual and group instruction across response tasks. *Journal of the Association for the Severely Handicapped 5*, 285-293.

Aherne, P. and Thornber, A. (1990) *Communication For All*, London, David Fulton.

Anderson, C.J. and Sawin, D. (1983) Enhancing responsiveness in mother-infant interaction. *Infant Behaviour and Development 6*, 361–368.

Aspin, P.N. (1982) Towards the concept of a human being as a basis for a philosophy for Special Education. *Education Review 34*, 113–123.

Barrera, M.E., Rosenbaum, P.L., and Cunningham, C.E. (1986) Early home intervention with low-birth-weight infants and their parents. *Child Development 57*, 20–33.

Bartlett, D. (1991) SATs for some but not for all. *British Journal of Special Education 18*, 90–92.

Bates, E., Benigni, L., Bretherton, I., Camaioni, L., and Volterra, V. (1979) *The Emergence of Symbols*, New York: Academic Press.

Baumgart, D. (1982) Principle of Partial Participation and individualized adaptations in educational programmes for severely handicapped students. *Journal of the Association for the Severely Handicapped 7* (2), 17–27.

Bayley, N. (1969) *Bayley Scales of Infant Development*, New York: The Psychological Corporation.

Behrmann, M.M. and Lahm, L. (1984) Babies and robots: Technology to assist learning of young multiply disabled children. *Rehabilitation Literature 45*, 194–201.

Belmont, J.M. (1989) Cognitive strategies and strategic learning. *American Psychologist 44*, 142–148.

Beveridge, M. and Berry, P. (1977) Observing interaction in the severely mentally handicapped, *Research in Education 17*, 14-22.

Blacher, J. (Ed.) (1984) *Severely Handicapped Young Children and Their Families*. New York: Academic Press.

Bovair, K. (1991) Introduction, in N. Ashdown, B. Carpenter and K. Bovair (Eds.) *The Curriculum Challenge*, London: Falmer Press.

Bray, A. (1988) Social interaction at home of young children with Down's Syndrome. Paper presented at the 8th IASSMD Congress Dublin August 1988.

Bremner, J.G. (1988) *Infancy*. Oxford: Blackwell.

Brinker, R.P. (1984) Curricula without recipes: a challenge to teachers and a promise to severely mentally retarded students. In D. Brinker and J. Filler, (Eds.) *Severe Mental Retardation. From Theory to Practice.* Preston, Virginia: Division Mental Retardation of the Council for Exceptional Children.

Brinker, R. P. (1985) Interactions between severely mentally retarded students and other students in integrated and segregated school settings. *American Journal of Mental Deficiency*, 89(6), 587–594.

Brinker, R.P. and Lewis, M.L. (1982) Discovering the competent handicapped infant: a process approach to assessment and intervention. *Topics in Early Childhood Special Education 2*, 1–16.

Brinker, R. P. and Thorpe, M.E. (1984) Integration of severely handicapped students and the proportion of IEP objectives achieved. *Exceptional Children 51*(2), 168–175.

Brown, F., Holvoet, J., Guess, D. and Mulligan, M. (1980) The individualised curriculum sequencing model III: Small group instruction. *Journal of the Association of the Severely Handicapped 5*, 352–367.

Bruner, J. (1983) *Child's Talk: Learning to Use Language.* New York: Norton.

Bruner, J.S. (1985) Vygotsky: A historical and conceptual perspective. In J.V. Wertsch (Ed) *Culture, Communication and Cognition: Vygotskian Perspectives.* Cambridge University Press.

Burford, B. (1986) Communication through movement, in Shanley, E. (Ed.) *Mental Handicap: A Handbook of Care.* London: Churchill Livingstone.

Burford, B. (1988) Action Cycles: Rhythmic actions for engagement with children and young adults with profound mental handicap. *European Journal of Special Needs Education, 3*, 189–206.

Carden, N. (1991) Planning National Curriculum science. *British Journal of Special Education 18*, 93–95.

Carpenter, B., Fathers, J., Lewis, A. and Privett, R. (1988) Integration: the Coleshill experience. *British Journal of Special Education 15*(3), 119–121.

Carpenter, B. and Lewis, A. (1989) Searching for solutions: Approaches to planning the curriculum for integration of SLD & PMLD children. In Baker, D. and Bovair, K. *Making the Special Schools Ordinary (vol. 1)*, London: Falmer Press.

Carpenter, B., Lewis, A. and Moore, J. (1986) Integration: a project involving young children with severe learning difficulties and first school children. *Mental Handicap 14*, 152–157.

Cole, D.A. (1986) Facilitating play in children's peer relationships: are we having fun yet? *American Educational Research Journal 23*(2), 201–215.

Cole, D.A. Vandercook, T. and Rynders, J. *Peer interaction programs for children with and without severe disabilities.* Unpublished paper.

Coles , E. and Blunden, R. (1979) The Establishment and Maintenance of a Ward-Based Activity Period within a Mental Handicap Hospital. *Research Report No 8* Cardiff: Mental Handicap in Wales Applied Research Unit.

Conti-Ramsden, G. and Taylor, G. (1990) Teacher-pupil talk: Integrated vs segregated environments for children with severe learning difficulties. *British Journal of Communication Disorders*, 25, 1–15.

Corbett, J. (1992) 'Totally impractical!' Integrating 'special care' within a special school. In Booth, T., Swann, W., Wasterton, M. and Potts, P. (Eds.) *Curricula for Diversity in Education.* Milton Keynes: OUP.

Cornell, B. and Carden, N. (1990) Principles must come first. *British Journal of Special Education 17*, 4–7.

Coupe O'Kane, J. and Baker, P. (1992) Editorial *SLD Experience 3*, 1.

Coupe, J. and Goldbart, J. (Eds.) (1988) *Communication Before Speech.* London: Croom Helm.

Coupe, J., Barton, L., Barber, M., Collins, L., Levy, D., and Murphy, D. (1985) *Affective Communication Assessment.* Manchester: MEC available from Melland School. Holmcroft Road M19 7NG.

Coupe, J., Barber, M. and Murphy, D. (1988) Affective communication. In J. Colupe, and J. Goldbart, (Eds.) *Communication Before Speech.* London: Croom Helm.

Crisp, A. and Sturmey, P. (1984) Organizing staff to promote purposeful activity in a setting for mentally handicapped adults: an evaluation of alternative strategies – small groups and room management. *Behavioural Psychotherapy 12*, 281-299.

Cunningham, C.C. and Glenn, S.M. (1986) Parent involvement and early intervention. In Stratford, B. and Lane, D. *Current Approaches to Down's Syndrome.* Eastbourne Holt, Rinehart, Winston.

Cunningham, C.E., Reuler, E., Blackwell, J. and Deck, J. (1981) Behavioural and linguistic development in the interactions of normal and retarded children with their mothers. *Child Development 52*, 62–70.

Dailey, W.F., Allen, G.J., Chinsky, J.M. and Viet, S.W. (1974) Attendant behaviour and attitudes toward institutionalised retarded children. *American Journal of Mental Deficiency 78*, 586–591.

Daniels H. and Ware J. (Eds.) (1990) *Special educational needs and the National Curriculum,* Bedford Way Series.

De Casper, A.J. and Carstens, A.A. (1981) Contingencies of stimulations: Effects on learning and emotion in neonates. *Infant Behaviour and Development 4*, 19–35.

Dearing, R. (1994) *The National Curriculum and its Assessment: Final Report*, London: SCAA.

Des/Welsh Office (1985) *The Organisation and Content of the Curriculum: Special Schools* (Note).

DES (1989) *From Policy to Practice.*

Dickinson, A. (1980) *Contemporary Animal Learning Theory*, Cambridge University Press.

Dunst, C.J. (1980) *A Clinical and Educational Manual for use with the Uzgiris and Hunt Scales of Infant Psychological Development.* Baltimore: University Park Press.

Dunst, C.J., Cushing, P.J. and Vance, S.D. (1985) Response-contingent learning in profoundly handicapped infants: A social systems perspective. *Analysis and Intervention in Developmental Disabilities 5*, 33–47.

Elbers, E. (1987) *Social Context and the Child's Construction of Knowledge.* Drukkerij Elinkwijk Br-Utrecht.

Ellis, A. and Beattie, G. (1986) *The Psychology of Language and Communication*, London: Weidenfeld and Nicolson.

Emblem B. and Conti-Ramsden G. (1990) Towards level 1: Reality or Illusion. *British Journal of Special Education 17*, 88–90.

Evans, P. and Ware, J. (1987) *Special Care Provision – The Education of Children with Profound and Multiple Learning Difficulties* and Windsor: NFER-Nelson.

Fagg S., Aherne P., Skelton S. and Thornber A. (1990) *Entitlement For All In Practice*, London: David Fulton.

Farouk, S. (1990) Curriculum for Children with SLDs. Unpublished Professional Educational Psychology Masters Report. University of London Institute of Education.

Felce, D., de Kock, U. and Repp, A. (1986) An eco-behavioral analysis of small community-based group houses and traditional large hospitals for severely and profoundly mentally handicapped adults. *Applied Research in Mental Retardation 7*, 393–408.

Felce, D. (1991) Using behavioural principles in the development of effective housing services for adults with severe or profound mental handicap. In B. Remington, (Ed.) *The Challenge of Severe Mental Handicap: A Behaviour Analytic Approach*, Chichester: Wiley.

Felce, D. and Perry, J. (1993) Quality of Life: A contribution to its definition and measurement. Paper presented at the Annual Conference of the British Institute for Learning Disabilities, Torquay, September 1993.

Fink, W. and Sandall, S. (1980) A comparison of one-to-one and small group instructional strategies with developmentally disabled pre-schoolers. *Mental Retardation 18* 34–35.

Finkelstein, N.W. and Ramey, C.T. (1977) Learning to control the environment in infancy. *Child Development 48*, 806–819.

Fish, J. Mongan, D., Evans, J. and Wedell (1987) *Memorandum to the DES in response to the consultation document on the national curriculum.* London University, Institute of Education, Library Archive collection, Ref 199/1987/88.

Fordham, D. (1989) Flexibility in the National Curriculum. *British Journal of Special Education 16*, 50–52.

Fuchs, L.S. and Fuchs, D. (1986) Linking assessment to instructional intervention: an overview. *School Psychology Review 15*(3), 318–323.

Gleason, J.J. (1990) Meaning of play: interpreting patterns in behavior of persons with severe developmental disabilities. *Anthropology and Education Quarterly 21*, 59–77.

Glenn, S.M. (1986) People with profound retardation and multiple impairment: a developmental perspective. Paper presented at Joint Mencap/RSM Conference on People with Profound Multiple Impairments, University of Manchester, UK, 25th September.

Glenn, S.M. (1988a) Interactive Approaches to working with children with profound and multiple learning difficulties. In B. Smith (Ed.) *Interactive Approaches to the Education of Children with Severe Learning Difficulties.* Birmingham, U.K. Westhill College.

Glenn, S.M. (1988b) Activities to encourage children's development within the early sensorimotor period. In Smith, B. (Ed.) *Interactive Approaches to the Education of Children with Severe Learning Difficulties.* Birmingham, U.K. Westhill College.

Glenn, S.M. and Cunningham, C.C. (1984) Selective auditory preferences and the use of automated equipment by severely profoundly and multiply handicapped children. *Journal of Mental Deficiency Research 28*, 281–296.

Glenn and O'Brien (this volume).

Goldbart, J. (1985) The assessment of programmed and environmental factors in teaching language to developmentally delayed children. Unpublishned PhD Thesis, University of Manchester.

Goldbart, J. (1990) Pre-intentional communication: Opening the communication curriculum to students with profound and multiple learning difficulties. Paper presented to *NCSE Special Education Congress, Cardiff*, August 1990.

Goldbart (this volume).

Goldbart, J. and Rigby, J. (1989) Establishing relationships with people with PMLD. Paper presented to University of Manchester Department of Child and Adolescent Psychiatry Regional Study Day, 10th April 1989.

Goldbart, J., Warner, J. and Mount, H. (1992) *Communication and Feeding: a workshop for parents and carers*, Manchester: Mencap PRMH Project, In Press.

Goodstein, H.A. (1982) Reliability of criterion referenced tests and special education: assumed versus demonstrated. *Journal of Special Education 16*, 37–48.

Gow, L., Balla, J. and Butterfield, E. (1990) The relative efficacy of cognitive and behavioural approaches to instruction in promoting adaptive capacity. In W. Fraser (Ed.) *Key Issues in Mental Retardation Research*, London: Routledge.

Grant, G. W. B. and Moores, B. (1977) Resident characteristics and staff behaviour in two hospitals for mentally retarded adults, *American Journal of Mental Deficiency 82*. 259–265.

Great Britain *Education Reform Act 1988.*

Griffiths, R. (1970) *Griffiths Scales of Mental Development.* Taunton: Child Development Centre.

Grove, N. and Park, K. (1994) *Odyssey Now*, obtainable from SENJIT, London University Institute of Education.

Guess, D. Mulligan-Ault, M., Roberts, S., Struth, J., Siegel-Causey, E., Thompson, B. Bronicki, G.J. and Guy, B. (1988) Implications of biobehavioral states for the education and treatment of students with the most profoundly handicapping Conditions. *Journal of the Association for Persons with Severe Handicaps 13*(3), 163–174.

Gunzberg, H.C. (1963) *Progress Assessment Charts*, London: NAMH.

Hanks, P. (Ed.) (1986) *Collins Dictionary of the English Language (2nd Edition)*, London: Collins.

Hanson, M.J. and Hanline, M.F. (1985) An analysis of response-contingent learning experiences for young children. *Journal of Association for Persons with Severe Handicaps 10*, 31–40.

Hanzlik, J. R. and Stevenson, M. B. (1986) Interaction of mothers with their infants who are mentally retarded, retarded with cerebral palsy, or nonretarded. *American Journal of Mental Deficiency 90*, 513–520.

Harding, C. G. (1982) Development of the intention to communicate. *Human Development*, 25, 140–151.

Harding, C. G. (1983) Setting the stage for language acquisition: communication development in the first year. In R. M. Golinkoff (Ed.) *The Transition from Prelinguistic to Linguistic Communication.* Hillsdale NJ: LEA.

Haring, T.G. and Breen, C. (1989) Units of social interaction outcomes in supported education. *Journal of the Association for Persons with Severe Handicaps 14*(4), 255–262.

Harrison, J., Lombardino, L. and Stapell, J. (1987) The development of early communication: using developmental literature for selecting communication goals *Journal of Special Education 20*, 263–473.

Hart, B. and Risley, T.R. (1976) Environmental reprogramming: Implications for the severely handicapped. Unpublished Paper. Kansas: Centre for Applied Behaviour Analysis.

Haskett, J. and Hollar, W.D. (1978) Sensory reinforcement and contingency awareness of profoundly retarded children. *American Journal of Mental Deficiency 83*, 60–68.

Hegarty, J.R. (1991) (Ed.) *The Present and Future of Microcomputers for People with Learning Difficulties.* Keele, Staffs: Change Publication.

Hewett, D. (1989) The most severe learning difficulties: Does your curriculum 'go back far enough?' In M. Ainscow (ed) *Special Education in Change*. London: David Fulton.

Hill, C.A. and Whiteley, J. H. (1986) Social interactions and on-task behaviour of severely multihandicapped and nonhandicapped children in mainstreamed classrooms. *Canadian Journal of Special Education 2*(2), 199–210.

Hogg, J., Lambe, L., Cowie, J. Coxon, J. (1987) *People with Profound Retardation And Multiple Handicaps Attending Schools or Social Education Centres.* Manchester:

Hogg, J. and Raynes, N. (Eds.) (1987) *Assessment in Mental Handicap*, London: Croom Helm.

Hogg, J. and Sebba, J. (1986) *Profound Retardation and Multiple Impairment, vols 1 and 2.* London: Croom Helm.

Holly, G. (1992) Letter dated 19.2.92 from Graham Holly (DES) to Christina Tilstone (Organiser Birmingham conference on assessment in the National Curriculum for pupils with severe learning difficulties) for circulation.

Johns, J. (1990) The Implications of the National Curriculum for Children and Students with PMLD. Unpublished Professional Educational Psychology Masters Report University of London Institute of Education.

Kahn, J.V. (1976) Utility of the Uzgiris and Hunt scales of sensorimotor development with severely and profoundly retarded children. *American Journal of Mental Deficiency 80*, 663–665.

Kahn, J. (1984) Cognitive training and initial use of referential speech. *Topics in Language Disorders 5*, 14–28.

Kaye, K. (1979) Thickening thin data: the maternal role in developing communication and language. In M. Bullowa (Ed.) *Before Speech*, Cambridge: CUP.

Kiernan, C. (1985) The Development of Communication and Cognition. In J. Dobbing (Ed.) *Scientific Studies in Mental Retardation*, Royal Society of Medicine/Macmillan Press.

Kiernan, C. and Jones, M.C. (1977, 1982) *The Behaviour Assessment Battery*, Windsor: NFER-Nelson.

Kingscote, S. (1992) Platform. *Eye Contact 3* Summer 1992, 1–2.

Knight, C. and Watson, J. 1990, Intensive Interactive Teaching at Gogarburn School, Moray House, Institute of Education (copies obtainable from the author).

Kohl, F.L., Moses, L.G. and Stettner-Eaton, B.A. (1984) A systematic training program for teaching nonhandicapped students to be instructional trainers of severely handicapped schoolmates. In Certo, N., Haring, N. and York, R. *Public School Integration of Severely Handicapped Students*, Baltimore: Paul H. Brookes.

La Mendola, Zaharia and O'Brien (1987) Foundation Care: A treatment model for non-ambulatory profoundly mentally retarded persons. *American Journal of Mental Deficiency 91*, 341–347.

Landesman-Dwyer, S. and Knowles, M. (1987) Ecological analysis of staff training in residential settings. In J. Hogg and P. Mittler (Eds.) *Staff Training in Mental Handicap*, Beckenham: Croom Helm.

Landesman-Dwyer, S. and Sackett, G. (1978) Behavioral Changes in nonambulatory profoundly mentally retarded individuals. In C.E. Meyers (Ed.) *Quality of Life in Severely and Profoundly Retarded People: Research Foundations for Improvement.* Washington DC: American Association on Mental Deficiency.

Lawson, D. and Chitty, C. (1988) *The National Curriculum.* Bedford Way Series. No. 33.

LeLaurin, K. and Riseley, T. (1972) The organization of day-care environments : 'Zone' versus 'man-to-man' staff assignments *Journal of Applied Behavior Analysis 5*, 225–232.

Lewis, A. (1991) Entitled to learn together? In R. Ashdown, B. Carpenter, and K. Bovair, *The Curriculum Challenge*, London: Falmer Press.

Lewis, A. and Carpenter, B. (1990) Discourse, in an integrated setting, between six and seven year old non-handicapped children and peers with severe learning difficulties. In Fraser, W. (Ed.), *Key Issues in Mental Retardation*, London: Routledge.

Lewis, M. and Coates, D.L. (1980) Mother-infant interactions and cognitive development in twelve-week-old infants. *Infant Behavior and Development 3*, 95–105.

Longhorn, F. (1988) *Planning a Sensory Curriculum for the Very Special Child*, London: Souvenir Press.

Lovett, S. (1985) Microelectronic and computer-based technology. In A.M. Clarke, A.D.B. Clarke and J.M. Berg (Eds.) *Mental Deficiency: the Changing Outlook*. 4th Ed. Methuen.

MacPherson, F.D. and Butterworth, G.E. (1981) Application of a Piagetian infant development scale to the assessment of profoundly mentally handicapped children. Paper presented to the Annual Conference. Developmental Psychology Section, British Psychological Society. Manchester U.K. Sept. 1981.

Macpherson, F. and Butterworth, G. (1988) Sensorimotor intelligence in severely mentally handicapped children. *Journal of Mental Deficiency Research 32*, 465–478.

Mahoney, G. and Powell, A. (1988) Modifying parent-child interaction: enhancing the development of handicapped children. *The Journal of Special Education 22*(1), 82–96.

Mahoney, G. and Robenalt, K. (1986) A comparison of conversational patterns between mothers and their Down syndrome and normal infants. *Journal of the Division for Early Childhood 10*(2), 172–180.

Mansell, J., Felce, D., Dekock, V., and Jenkins, J. (1982) Increasing purposeful activity of severely and profoundly handicapped adults, *Behaviour Research and Therapy 20*. 593–604.

Mansell, J., Felce, D., Jenkins, J. and Dekock, U., (1982) Increasing staff ratios in an activity with severely mentally handicapped people. *British Journal of Mental Subnormality 28*, 97–99.

McBrien, J. and Weightman, J. (1980) The effect of room management procedures on the engagement of profoundly retarded children. *British Journal of Mental Subnormality 26* 38–46.

McCollum, J.A. (1984) Social interaction between parents and babies: Validation of an intervention model. *Child: Care, Health and Development 10*, 301–315.

McConkey, R. (1990) Play and Games: Building up a Human Heritage, in *Scottish Concern*, November, National Children's Bureau.

McLean, J. and Snyder-Mclean, L. (1987) Form and function of communicative behaviour among persons with severe developmental disabilities. *Australia and New Zealand Journal of Developmental Disabilities 13* 83–98.

Mitchell, D.R. (1986) Medical treatment of severely impaired infants in New Zealand hospitals, *New Zealand Medical Journal 99*, 364–368.

Mitchell, D.R. (1987) Parents' interactions with their developmentally disabled or at risk infants – A Focus for Intervention. Invited Paper to the *New Zealand Journal of Developmental Disabilities*.

Mundy, P., Seibert, J. and Hogan, A., (1984) Relationship between sensorimotor and early communication abilities in developmentally delayed children, *Merrill-Palmer Quarterly*, 30, 33–48.

Naglieri, J.A. (1981) Extrapolated Developmental Indices for the Bayley Scales of Infant Development, *American Journal of Mental Deficiency 85*, 548–550.

National Curriculum Council (1992) *Curriculum Guidance Nine*, York: National Curriculum Council.

National Curriculum Council (1993) *Special Needs and the National Curriculum: Opportunity and Challenge*, York: National Curriculum Council.

Newson, J. (1978) Dialogue and development. In A. Locke (Ed.) *Action, Gesture and Symbol: the emergence of language.* New York: Academic Press.

Newson, J. (1979) The growth of shared understandings between infant and caregiver. In M. Bullowa (Ed.) *Before Speech.* Cambridge: CUP.

Nind, M. (1993) Access To Communicating: Efficacy Of Intensive Interaction Teaching For People With Severe Developmental Disabilities Who Demonstrate Autistic Behaviours. Unpublished PhD thesis, University of East Anglia.

Nind, M. and Hewett, D. (1988) Interaction as a curriculum. *British Journal of Special Education 15*, 55–57.

Norwich, B. (1990) How should we define exceptions? *British Journal of Special Education 16*, 95–97.

Norwich, B. (In Press) The National Curriculum and special educational needs. In J. White (Ed.) Bedford Way Paper.

Norwich, B. (1990) *Reappraising Special Needs Education*, London: Cassell.

O'Brien, Y. and Glenn, S.M. (1989) Factors affecting the demonstration of contingency responding and awareness in infancy. Paper presented at Annual B.P.S. Conference, April 1989, St Andrews, Scotland.

O'Brien, Y., Pollard, P. and Mullin, C. (1989) Computer-controlled equipment for the study of contingency learning in infancy. Unpublished paper. Available School of Psychology, Lancashire Polytechnic, Preston, PR1 2TQ, U.K.

O'Connell (this volume).

Odor, J.P. (1988) Student models in machine-mediated learning. *Journal of Mental Deficiency Research 32*, 247–256.

Oswin, M. (1978) *Children in Long Stay Hospitals*, Harmondsworth: Penguin.

Ouvry, C. (1986) Integrating pupils with profound and multiple handicaps. *Mental Handicap 14*, 157–160.

Ouvry, C. (1987) *Educating Children with Profound Handicaps*, Kidderminster: BIMH.

Ouvry, C. (1991) Access for pupils with profound and multiple learning difficulties. In N. Ashdown, B. Carpenter and K. Bovair (Eds.) *The Curriculum Challenge*, Falmer Press, London.

Owens, R.E. (1988) *Language Development: An Introduction.* Columbus Ohio: Charles Merrill 2nd ed.

Paton, X. and Stirling, E. (1974) Frequency and type of dyadic nurse-patient verbal interactions in a mental subnormality hospital. *International Journal of Nursing Studies 11*, 135–145.

Peter, M. (1989) National Curriculum: a year's grace. *British Journal of Special Education 16*(1) 18.

Piaget, J. (1952) *The Origins of Intelligence in Children.* New York: International University Press.

Pope, C. (1988) Room Management with target setting in a classroom for pupils with severe mental handicaps. *Mental Handicap Research 1*, 186–196.

Porterfield, J. (1982) Client participation. *Mental Handicap 10*, 94–95.

Porterfield, J. and Blunden, R. (1978) Establishing an activity period and individual skill training within a day setting for profoundly mentally handicapped adults. *Research Report No. 6* Cardiff: Mental Handicap in Wales Applied Research Unit.

Posner, G.J. and Strike, K.A. (1976) A categorization scheme for principles of sequencing content. *Review of Educational Research 46*(4). 665–690.

Pratt, M. Bumstead, D. and Raynes, N. (1976) Attendent staff speech to the institutionalized retardate: language use as a measure of the quality of care, *Journal of Psychology and Psychiatry 17*, 133–143.

Rainforth, B. (1982) Biobehavioral state and orienting: Implications for educating profoundly retarded student. *Journal of the Association for the Severely Handicapped 6*, 33–37.

Remington, B. and Evans, J. (1988) Basic learning processes in people with profound mental handicap: research and relevance. *Mental Handicap Research 1*, 4–23.

Remington, R.E., Foxen, R. and Hogg, J. (1979) Auditory reinforcement in profoundly retarded multiple handicapped children. *American Journal of Mental Deficiency 82*, 299–304.

Reynell, J. (1979) *Reynell-Zinkin Scales for Young Visually Handicapped Children.* Windsor, Berks: NFER Publishing Co.

Rogers, S.J. (1977) Characteristics of the cognitive development of profoundly retarded children. *Child Development 48*, 837–843.

Rose, R. (1991) A jigsaw approach to group work. *British Journal of Special Education 18*(2), 54–58.

Sandhu, J. (1983) *The use of Microelectronics in Education of ESN(s) Children*, Handicapped Persons Research Unit. Newcastle Polytechnic.

Saxby, H., Felce, D., Harman, M. and Repp, A. (1988) The maintenance of client activity and staff-client interaction in small community houses for severely handicapped adults: A two year follow-up, *Behavioural Psychotherapy 16*, 189–206.

Schulz, K. (1993) Hungarian paediatricians' attitudes regarding the treatment and non-treatment of defective newborns. A comparative study. *Bioethics* 7(1), 41–56.

Schweigert, P. (1989) Use of microswitch technology to facilitate social contingency awareness as a basis for early communication skills. *Augmentative and Alternative Communication*, 5, 192–198.

Scoville, R. (1984) Development of the intention to communicate: The eye of the beholder. In Feagens, L., Garvey, C., and Golinkoff, R. (1984) (Eds.) *The Origins and Growth of Communication.* NJ Ablex Publishing Corporation.

Sebba, J., Byers, R. and Rose, R. (1993) *Redefining the Whole Curriculum for Pupils with Learning Difficulties*, London: David Fulton.

Seligman, M. (1975) *Helplessness: On Depression, Development and Death.* San Francisco: Freeman.

Sharpe, P. (1993) Paper presented at the London Conference of the British Psychological Society. City University December 1993.

Shepherd, P.A. and Fagan, J.F. (1981) Visual pattern detection and recognition memory in children with profound mental retardation. In N.R. Ellis (Ed.) *International Review of Research in Mental Retardation 10*, 31–60.

Singer, P. (1985) Can we avoid assigning greater value to some human lives than others? In R. Laura and A. Ashman (Eds.) *Moral Issues in Mental Retardation*. Beckenham: Croom Helm.

Snow, C., Dubber, C. and de Blaauw, A. (1982) Routines in mother-child interaction. In Feagens, L. and Forroni, D.C. (Eds.) *The Language of Children Raised in Poverty.* (pp 53–74) New York: Academic Press.

Soder, M. (1989) Disability as a social construct: the labelling approach revisited. *European Journal of Special Educational Needs 4*(2), 117–129.

Stern, D. (1977) *The First Relationship: Infant and Mother.* London: Fontana/Open Books.

Sternberg, L. and Richards, S. (1989) Assessing levels of state and arousal in individuals with profound handicaps: a research integration. *Journal of Mental Deficiency Research 33*, 381–387.

Storm, R. and Willis, J. (1978) Small group training as an alternative to individual programmes for profoundly retarded persons. *American Journal of Mental Deficiency 83*, 283–288.

Sugarman, S. (1984) The development of preverbal communication. In R.L. Schiefelbusch and J. Peckar (Eds.) *The Acquisition of Communicative Competence.* Baltimore: University Park Press.

Switzky, H.N. and Rotatori, A.F. (1981) Assessment of perceptual cognitive functioning in nonverbal severely and profoundly handicapped children. *Early Child Development and Care 7*, 29–44.

Terdal, L.E., Jackson, R.H. and Garner, A.M. (1976) Mother-child interactions: A comparison between normal and developmentally delayed groups. In E.J. Mash, L.A. Hamerlynck and L.C. Handy (Eds.) *Behaviour Modification and Families*, New York: Brunner/Mazel.

Tilstone, C. (1991) *Teaching Children with Severe Learning Difficulties: Practical Approaches*, London: Fulton.

Utley, B.L., Zigmond, N. and Strain, P.S. (1987) How various forms of data affect teacher analysis of student performance. *Exceptional Children 53*, 411–422.

Uzgiris, I. and Hunt, J.McV. (1975) *Assessment in Infancy: Ordinal Scales of Psychological Development*, Urbana: University of Illinois Press.

Voeltz, L. H. (1982) Effects of structured interactions with severely handicapped peers on children's attitudes. *American Journal of Mental Deficiency 86*(4), 380–390.

Vygotsky, L.S. (1978) *Mind in Society: The Development of Higher Psychological Processes.* Cambridge: Harvard University Press.

Wallwork, A.S. (1986) Chance or Choice? – Can students with profound and very severe learning difficulties express preferences by activating switches? Unpublished M. Ed. thesis, Exeter University, U.K.

Ware, J. (1987) Providing Education for Children with Profound and Multiple Learning Difficulties: A Survey of Resources and an Analysis of Staff:Pupil Interactions in Special Care Units. Unpublished PhD Thesis University of London Institute of Education.

Ware, J. (1990a) Interactions between pupils with severe learning difficulties and non-handicapped peers. *Reach 4*(1), 44–48.

Ware, J. (1990b) Designing appropriate environments for people with profound and multiple learning difficulties. In Fraser, W. (Ed) *Key Issues in Mental Retardation*, London: Routledge.

Ware, J. (1990c) The National Curriculum for pupils with severe learning difficulties. In H. Daniels and J. Ware (Eds.) *Special Educational Needs and the National Curriculum: The Impact of the Education Reform Act*, Bedford Way Paper London: Kogan Page/Institute of Education.

Ware, J. (1992) Working Towards: Dilemma or Opportunity? Unpublished paper presented at a Conference held at the Institute of Education, 16th October 1992.

Ware, J. (This volume)

Ware, J. and Evans, P.L. (1986) Interactions between profoundly handicapped pupils and staff in a special care class. In Berg, J.M. and De Jong, J. (Eds.) *Science and Service in Mental Retardation.* London: Methuen.

Ware, J. and Evans, P. (1987) Room Management is not enough? *British Journal of Special Education 14.*

Ware, J. and Evans, P. (1988) Allowing for dialogue? Observing interactions between children and staff in 'special care' classes. Unpublished paper.

Warren, S.F., Alpert, C.L. and Kaiser A.R. (1986) An optimal learning environment for infants and toddlers with severe handicaps. *Focus on Exceptional Children 18*, 1–11.

Warren, S.F. and Horne, M. (1987) Microcomputer applications in early childhood special education: Problems and possibilities. *Topics in Early Childhood Special Education 7*, 72–84.

Watson, J. (This volume).

Watson, J.S. (1967) Memory and contingency analysis in infant learning. *Merrill-Palmer Quarterly 13*, 55–76.

Watson, J.S. (1972) Smiling, cooing and the game. *Merrill-Palmer Quarterly 18*, 323–329.

Watson, J.S., Hayes, L.A. and Vietze, P. (1982) Response contingent stimulation as a treatment for developmental failure in infancy. *Journal of Applied Developmental Psychology 3*, 191–203.

Watson, J.S. and Ramey, C.T. (1972) Reactions to response-contingent stimulation in early infancy. *Merrill-Palmer Quarterly 18*, 219–227.

Watts, T. (1991) The role of the computer with children who have profound learning difficulties. In J.R. Hegarty (Ed.) *The Present and Future of Microcomputers for People with Learning Difficulties.* Change Publications, 27–37.

Webster, A. and Webster, V. (1990) *Profiles of Development: Recording Children's progress within the National Curriculum*, Bristol: Avec Designs.

Wedell, K. (1981) Concepts of special educational need. *Education Today 31*, 3–9.

Welsh Office (1994) Draft Circular XX/94 (The Future Development of Special Schools).

Westling, D.L., Ferrell, K. and Swenson, K. (1982) Intraclass comparison of two arrangements for teaching profoundly mentally retarded children. *American Journal of Mental Deficiency 86*, 601–608.

Wetherby, A., Cain, D., Yonclas, D., and Walker, V. (1988) Analysis of intentional communication of normal children from the prelinguistic to the multiword stage, *JSHR*, 31, 240–252.

White, J. (1991) The goals are the same ... or are they? *British Journal of Special Education 18(1)*, 25–27.

Whiteley, J.H. and Krenn, M.J. (1986) Uses of the Bayley Scales with non-ambulatory profoundly mentally retarded children. *American Journal of Mental Deficiency 90*, 425–431.

Williams, C. (1978) An introduction to behavioural principles in teaching the profoundly handicapped. *Child: Care, Health and Development*, Vol 4(1) 21–27.

Woodward, M. (1959) The behaviour of idiots interpreted by Piaget's theory of sensori-motor development. *British Journal of Educational Psychology 29*, 60–71.

Yoder, P. (1978) Relationship between degree of infant handicap and clarity of infant cues. *American Journal of Mental Deficiency 91*, 639–641.

Yoshida, R.K. (1984) Microcomputer technology and related services. *Special Services in the Schools 1*, 46–61.

Index